THE VISION OF CHRIST IN ST. COLUMBA CHURCH BROOKLYN

N. J. Azzaro M.S.

ISBN: 1976237777
ISBN 13: 9781976237775
Library of Congress Control Number: 2017914660
CreateSpace Independent Publishing Platform
North Charleston, South Carolina

Take care and be earnestly on your guard not to forget the things which your own eyes have seen, nor let them slip from your memory as long as you live, but teach them to your children's children. (Deuteronomy 4:9)

The life which is unexamined is not worth living. (Socrates)

The word of the Lord came to me thus: Before I formed you in the womb, I knew you... (Jeremiah 1:5)

Grace and truth came through Jesus Christ. (John 1:17)

INTRODUCTION

This is my story, my spiritual memoir. It's a little strange but it's mine and I have to own it. This book tells my personal story of an unusual, spiritual-religious experience I had many years ago. Elements of the mystical and supernatural are woven into the story, because that was my experience. We don't always get to choose what happens to us in life, some things just happen and we have no control over them. If you are an open-minded person, if you believe in God and in the mystical, mysterious and the supernatural you'll find my story interesting. You'll also have to believe in the existence of the unseen, invisible, intangible, but very real dimension where God exists. There are other dimensions, other than the three-dimensional world we are aware of. I am convinced of that. If you believe in Christ as the Anointed One-Who is the Divine Son and God, this book should be a source of affirmation for you.

The mystery of the Blessed Trinity is the "central mystery" and most "essential" teaching for Christians, according to Church teaching and the *Catechism of the Catholic Church*. The doctrine of the Trinity has its basis in Scripture, from words that Jesus spoke. Jesus said: *The Father and I are one (John 10:30)*. Jesus also spoke to his apostles and disciples of the coming of the Holy Spirit. He told them "the Comforter," "the Advocate," would come after he ascended and remind them of all that he said and did. He promised the Holy Spirit would empower them and give them courage. The Spirit did all that and much more. Jesus said, before he ascended into Heaven:

> *You will receive power when the Holy Spirit comes upon you…..and you will be my witnesses in Jerusalem, throughout Judea and Samaria and to the ends of the earth (Acts 1:8).*

All of that happened as Jesus promised.

Christians believe in One God in Three Divine Persons: Father, Son and Holy Spirit. The Trinity has been described as a community of love, in which we are called to participate. The Trinity has also been referred to as a "round dance" of love. Christians strive to encounter the mystery of the Holy Trinity with love, openness and receptivity. The only way, according to the mystics, to gain insights into the mystery of God (which will always be limited) and to pierce the mystery is through love, prayer (especially contemplation) and the prayerful study and reflection of Scripture.

This book is about Jesus, whose name means "God saves." Jesus' name states his purpose as Savior. Jesus is a loving and merciful Savior. The many exalted titles of Jesus remind us that Jesus is: Redeemer, Eternal Wisdom, the Holy One of God, the Christ, the Lord, the Divine Physician, the True Light, the Lamb of God, the Alpha and Omega, the Son of God and God. In Aramaic, (the language spoken by Jesus and throughout the Middle East at the time Jesus lived) the word for Jesus is Jeshua or Yeshua. The Hebrew root "shua" means, "to save." Christ (in Greek: Christos) means the Anointed One of God. In Hebrew, "anointed one," means Messiah. The early Christians called Jesus, after the Resurrection-the Christ. Since the title "Christ" identifies Jesus as the Messiah, it is considered the most important title. It is also the root of the name "Christian," as His followers would be called.

Jesus' followers would also use a phrase in their communal gatherings, "Jesus is Lord!" "Jesus is Kyrios!" (Kyrios is Greek for Lord.) They proclaimed Jesus as "Lord of the Universe."

Jesus is the Second "Person" of the Holy Trinity, the Son of God and God. The Church teaches and Christians profess that Jesus is fully human and fully divine. Jesus fully possesses the divine nature with the Father and the Holy Spirit. For Christians, Jesus is the fullness and completeness of God's revelation. The Bible teaches that we are made in the image and likeness of God and so we can be open to God's divine revelation. All of these mysteries are greater than the human mind can comprehend. Divine mysteries cannot be fully understood and perhaps they weren't meant to be. Yet, through the power of the Holy Spirit, and with faith, trust and love, Christian believers try to remain faithful to the revealed truth of the Holy Trinity-Three Divine "Persons" in **one God**. It's mind-boggling but over two billion Christians (of all denominations), throughout the world, profess it and accept it with faith.

Our knowledge about Jesus' life and teachings come from the *New Testament* writings, most especially the *Synoptic Gospels* (Matthew, Mark and Luke), *The Gospel of John* (the most mystical and cosmic of the gospels) and the *Letters of St. Paul.* (*The Acts of the Apostles*, a continuation and second volume of *St. Luke's Gospel*, tells the story of the early Church.) Also, Christians learned much about Jesus (doctrines were formulated over centuries) from the tradition of the early Church, from theologians, including the writings of the early Fathers of the Church, popes, the first councils and the private revelations of saints.

Christians trust the words of Sacred Scripture (both the *Hebrew Scriptures* and the *New Testament*) as the Word of God, divinely inspired and revealing divine truths. The Catholic Church accepts 46 books of the *Hebrew Scriptures* (the *Old Testament*) and 27 books of the *New Testament* as inspired and part of the canon of Scripture. The Word of God ("the Sword of the Spirit") is "food" for the mind and soul and Christians are spiritually "fed" by Holy Scripture and guided by its religious truths. The writers of Sacred Scripture were inspired by the Holy Spirit and we too should be inspired when we read or listen to the Scriptures. The word inspiration comes from the Latin root, "inspirare," which means "to breathe into." Christ is present in his Word and "speaks" to us through it. There will be many quotes from Scripture in this book from both the *Hebrew Scriptures* and the *New Testament*. (The *Hebrew Scriptures* are often referred to as the *Old Testament*, but in my writing they shall always be called the *Hebrew Scriptures*.) The Second Vatican Council (1962-1965) stated that the *Hebrew Scriptures* shed light on the *New Testament* and help us to understand it more fully. It is an important part of God's revelation. *The Old Testament is an indispensable part of Sacred Scripture. Its books are divinely inspired and retain a 'permanent value,' for the Old Covenant has never been revoked* (see *Catechism of the Catholic Church #121*).

Christians believe that the ancient prophecies spoken and written down in the *Hebrew Scriptures* have been fulfilled in Jesus as recorded in the *New Testament*.

Your Word is a lamp to guide me and a light for my path (Psalm 119:105).

Thus says the Lord: Just as from the heavens rain and snow come down and do not return there til they have watered the earth, making it fertile and fruitful, giving seed to the one who sows and bread to the one who eats, so shall my word be that goes forth from my mouth; my word shall not return to me void, but shall do my will, achieving the end for which I sent it (Isaiah 55:10-11).

New Testament passages which stress the importance of God's word:

The word of God is living and effective, sharper than any two-edge sword, penetrating even between soul and spirit, joints and marrow, and able to discern reflections and thoughts of the heart (Hebrews 4:12).

All Scripture is inspired by God and is useful for teaching, for refutation, for correction and for training in righteousness, so that one who belongs to God may be competent, equipped for every good work (2 Timothy 3:16-17).

Let the word of Christ dwell in you richly (Col. 3:16).

Christians are strengthened by the stories, personal witness accounts and testimony of the apostles, disciples

and the early Christians, as stated in the *New Testament.*
St. John would proclaim:

> *You, Lord, have the words of everlasting life. We*
> *have come to believe and are convinced that you are the*
> *Holy One of God (John 6:68-69).*

From *The First Letter of John* these powerful words affirming Christ:

> *What was from the beginning, what we have heard,*
> *what we have seen with our eyes, what we looked upon*
> *and touched with our hands concerns the Word of Life-*
> *for the life was made visible; we have seen it and testify*
> *to it and proclaim to you the eternal life that was with*
> *the Father and was made visible to us- What we have*
> *seen and heard we proclaim now to you, so that you too*
> *may have fellowship with us; for our fellowship is with*
> *the Father and with his Son, Jesus Christ We are writ-*
> *ing this so that our joy may be complete (1 John 1:1-4).*

The Word of God and the oral and written accounts of the ancient Christians, (some were martyred for their unwavering faith in Christ), have given hope and encouragement to Christians throughout the centuries.

Catholic Christians rely on Sacred Scripture as well as Sacred Tradition to guide them and help them understand God's revelation.

Therefore, brothers, stand firm and hold fast to the traditions that you were taught, either by an oral statement or by a letter of ours (2 Thessalonians 2:15).

Jesus, the Eternal Word, has remained through the centuries a compelling figure, larger than life. He is an enigma for some, a revered prophet for others, but for Christians Jesus was God incarnate, the long awaited Messiah. *Time Magazine* stated: *Jesus has left a bigger historical footprint in the world than any person who has ever existed.* According to Scripture, Jesus was the pre-existent *Word made flesh, who dwelt among us.*

In the beginning was the Word and the Word was with God, and the Word was God. He was in the beginning with God. All things came to be through Him and without him nothing came to be.... (John 1:1-3).

And the Word became flesh and made his dwelling among us, and we saw his glory, the glory as of the Father's only Son, full of grace and truth (John 1:14).

He is the image of the invisible God, the firstborn of all creation. For in Him were created all things in heaven and on the earth,..... All things were created through Him and for Him (Col. 1:15-16).

Catholics believe that Jesus continues to reign in Heaven and is the Divine head of the Catholic Church (while the pope is the human leader and head of the Church on earth).

This book is about Jesus, but it's also about me and you, the reader. I hope my story engages you, helps you on your own spiritual journey and most importantly gives you hope. This book is about a private revelation, a mystical experience, I had many years ago, when I was a young mother living in Brooklyn, raising my children and leading an "ordinary" life, as a Catholic wife, mother and spiritual seeker.

One of the reasons I'm writing this book is to try and find answers and make sense of my experiences. Why me? Why would I be the recipient of a private revelation from God? I wasn't overly religious at the time of the experience I will describe in this book. I didn't live in a convent, I didn't spend hours in prayer (what mother can?), but I did pray often and I was on a spiritual quest. I was a baptized and confirmed Catholic, I attended Church, read the Bible often as well as other spiritual and religious books. I volunteered in my Church's religious education program as a catechist, but that certainly wasn't anything unusual. But apparently it was enough. The whole story doesn't make any sense in the natural world, but God's ways are different from our ways. God answers to no one. God is God and God throughout salvation history has revealed Himself to imperfect, flawed and frail human beings, showing up at the most unexpected times. That's true but it's not clear why.

The reality is God can and God does sometimes pierce through our world, right in the midst of everyday life and ordinariness. That's what happened to me, just like that, for no apparent reason, though I was an unlikely choice, God chose to act. We are suppose to have childlike trust in God. The saints tells us to come to God with empty hands. We cannot understand God's mysterious ways. God will always be incomprehensible mystery. Many theologians and biblical scholars have said, "Who are we to question God or God's ways?" They're right. (Job from *The Book of Job* in the *Hebrew Scriptures* tried to question God and he was put in his place!) Through the great Hebrew Prophet Isaiah, God spoke these words:

> *For my thoughts are not your thoughts, nor are your ways my ways, says the Lord. As high as the heavens are above the earth, so high are my ways above your ways and my thoughts above your thoughts... (Isaiah 55:8-9).*

In some sense, I sometimes think of myself as a "victim," a "victim" of God's self-revelation. I'm sure God doesn't see it that way and I don't mean any disrespect. But the experiences altered my life (there was more than one) and changed me. I wasn't the same person afterwards. How could I be? I had what I believed were supernatural experiences and they were difficult to process and reflect upon. They were unsettling in many ways, and though I didn't tell anyone and I went on living an ordinary life, but with a changed view of reality. In some sense, my freedom was taken away.

When I think about the unusual experiences I've had in my life, which I did not seek and for which I was totally unprepared, I am still unnerved by it all, which is why I've put off telling this story for so long. I found out what it meant to be awestruck, by experiencing it. I didn't ask for, pray for, practice fasting, drink too much coffee or take any drugs or medications, which would have affected my state of mind or consciousness. I didn't even know it was possible for an ordinary Christian to have extraordinary religious, mystical experiences, except for the well known visionaries and I certainly wasn't in their category. I thought mystical experiences were for the holiest of saints who were cloistered nuns, blessed children, ascetical monks, prophets or priests. As a matter of fact I didn't know what the word mysticism or mystic meant. I never heard the word mentioned or explained in Church or catechism class. I would have to research and study the meaning of the word mystic and mysticism in depth, on my own, to try to make some sense of my experiences. I also studied the phenomena of mysticism at Fordham University, as part of my graduate religious studies there. (Even beginning graduate studies in religion, in my adult years, was to try to learn more and bring some validation of my experiences, if that was even possible.) I was afraid to discuss them with anyone. I didn't want to be ridiculed.

The one account I will describe and reflect upon in this book is a true story, a very personal account of one of my experiences, with a lot of reflection. You'll have to take my word, that to the best of my knowledge, the experience I will describe was an authentic religious experience. It was a very sacred, subjective and personal experience, which captivated my senses and opened another reality to me. The three-dimensional world we live in expanded before my eyes. That was something I didn't think was possible, I never gave it a second thought. It wasn't logical, but it happened anyway. The particular experience I will describe (and the few others I've had) were experiences I could never dismiss or forget about. Religious experiences leave an indelible mark on the mind and the soul. I had to make some sense of my life, and use my rational mind and intelligence to try to find an explanation. I had to confront the questions head on: Could I be a mystic? Could mystics be ordinary people? Could a mystic be living in a middle-class neighborhood in Brooklyn, right in the heart of New York City, not knowing they were a mystic, until experiences starting happening that were unexplainable in the natural world? (It sounds like fiction, it's not.) I may never know all the answers this side of Heaven but I've spent a lot of time delving into it. As a practicing Catholic and an avid reader, as I've mentioned, I was aware (before my experiences and research) of mystical saints, visionaries and private revelations, but not in my wildest dreams did I think it could happen to me or someone I knew, for that matter.

Some readers might be wondering why I didn't seek spiritual direction. Whenever I thought about seeking out a spiritual director, I became anxious. "What would I say?" "I've seen a vision of the risen Christ." I had read the writings of the great Carmelite mystic, St. John of the Cross. He wrote the following regarding mystical experience: *We should pay no heed to them, but be only interested in seeking God, with fortitude.*

Some private revelations have been thoroughly investigated and then approved by the Church, others have not. The visionaries of Medjugorje and their apparent messages from Mary are still being investigated by the Catholic Church. Those Marian apparitions still wait for approval from the Church, even as Catholics from around the world continue to make pilgrimages to the site. Catholics are not required to believe in private revelations, even ones that have been approved by the Church. They are not part of the deposit of faith.

There is a difference between public revelation and private revelation. According to the Church, public revelation ended with Jesus Christ and the *New Testament* writings. Public revelation (the deposit of faith) can never be contradicted by private revelation.

Two well known approved apparitions of Mary, took place in Europe. One extraordinary event happened in Lourdes, France and the other in Fatima, Portugal. The accounts of the visionary from Lourdes and the visionaries of Fatima are fascinating and worth reading about. In 1858, at the age of fourteen, young, sickly Bernadette Soubirous would experience eighteen visions of the Blessed Mother at the Grotto of Massabielle. Mary would reveal herself as "the Immaculate Conception," and ask for continual prayers for the conversion of sinners. Eventually Bernadette became a nun and remained humble all her life. She died in 1879 and was canonized a saint in 1933. The Shrine of Our Lady of Lourdes in France attracts millions of pilgrims each year and the number of visitors continues to grow.

In 1917, in Fatima, three young shepherd children (Lucia de Santos, Jacinta and Francisco Marto) experienced six visions of Mary. Many supernatural events took place at the time. Over 100,000 people witnessed the sun dance in the sky, ("The Miracle of the Sun") which was an extraordinary, cosmic sign from God. Mary revealed herself as "Our Lady of the Rosary," and asked the visionaries and others to say the rosary for the conversion of sinners and the conversion and consecration of Russia to her Immaculate Heart. The 100th Anniversary of the Marian apparitions of Our Lady of Fatima is being celebrated in 2017. On May 13th, a hundred years after Mary appeared to the three children, Pope Francis canonized Jacinta and her brother Francisco (who both died young), during Mass in Fatima. They are the youngest non-martyr saints ever canonized in the Church. Portuguese Cardinal Saraiva Martins, former prefect of the Congregation for Saints' Causes explained why they were canonized, "It was the children's heroism in their lives, their life of prayer, their turning to God that was truly holy."

Lucia, the only visionary of the three who lived to adulthood, became a Carmelite nun. She died in 2005 at the age of 97. Her cause for beatification is being investigated and is nearly complete.

Christians from around the world make pilgrimages to these holy shrines each year (and many others) and are edified by their experience. Some pilgrims report miraculous healings, which are then verified by medical doctors.

When it comes to discerning private revelations the Church is very careful and prudent, as she should be. When private revelations are finally approved, it is only after an exhaustive and thorough investigation. When a private revelation is found to be credible, the Church declares that it gives "evidence of a supernatural intervention" and is worthy of belief. Popes, at times, will encourage the faithful to acknowledge and be inspired by approved private revelations. For example, Pope St. John XXIII, declared that popes "have a duty to recommend to the attention of the faithful, when after mature examination they consider it opportune for the general good, the supernatural lights which it has pleased God to dispense freely to certain privileged souls, not to propose new doctrines but to guide our conduct" (Centenary of the apparitions at Lourdes).

I am not comparing my private revelation to any other. (People of faith can have mystical experiences without being saints, as I will try to explain many times in this book.) But obviously, my experience is important to me, to my life story and my spiritual journey. I have never sought to make my revelations known. I feel uncomfortable doing so, even now. I've neglected the writing of this book for months at a time because it's difficult for me to share this. But maybe this revelation I'm sharing will be of interest to someone, maybe it will increase faith in God and encourage belief. For that reason, I've picked it up once more. Also, after attending a Day of Prayer which included Eucharistic Adoration, on Divine Mercy Sunday in the Jubilee Year of Mercy (2016), I felt strongly that it is God's will that I complete this work.

Sometimes things are not what they seem. If you believe that God is real and that God has, at times, throughout salvation history, unexpectedly pierced through our world and revealed to ordinary people (as well as to some not-so-ordinary prophets and saints) aspects of God's divinity and nature, then this book should be of interest to you. Truth stands the test of time.

Regarding my worthiness, or anyone's worthiness to receive an authentic private revelation from God..... **No one is worthy**! It's a great mystery why God chooses certain people for extraordinary experiences. I have tried through good works and prayer to show my gratefulness to God, but no amount of good could equal the abundance of grace, mercy and private revelation I was given. This book is for Christians and all spiritual seekers to read, to give them hope, to help them on their own spiritual journey. God is a God of love as well as truth, goodness, forgiveness, mercy and great humility.

The Lord, the Lord, a merciful and gracious God, slow to anger and rich in kindness and fidelity (Ex. 34:6).

God's mercy and love for us is beyond our comprehension. God's mercy and unconditional love makes the impossible, possible. *With God all things are possible!* (See *Luke 1:37*)

God is real. From what I experienced I can write with certainty, that Jesus is who He said He was. He is the Christ. I was given a special grace to see deeply into truth. I truly believe that. I recognized the time of my visitation. I fully understand the seriousness of what I am about to write. I pray that it is God's will that I do so. To God be the glory forever.

N.J. Milone Azzaro

⊶✠⊷

Note: I entrust this work to Mary, under her title- Our Lady of Mount Carmel and place my efforts under her patronage.

Unless you become like little children, you shall not enter the kingdom of God. (Matthew 18:3)

None of us suddenly becomes something overnight. The preparations have been in the making for a lifetime. (Gail Godwin)

For I know well the plans I have in mind for you, says the Lord, plans for your welfare, not for woe! Plans to give you a future full of hope. When you call me, when you go to pray to me, I will listen to you. (Jeremiah 29:11-12)

The glory of God is a human being fully alive. (St. Irenaeus)

CHAPTER 1

EAST 52ND STREET, BROOKLYN, NEW YORK

I spent most of my childhood growing up on East 52nd Street in the Old Mill Basin section of Brooklyn. Before that, I spent the first two years of my life, with my parents, Mimi and Joey, living in an apartment in Coney Island, near Surf Avenue. My mother constantly reminded me that I was a poor eater, as a baby and toddler. She told me, (when I was old enough to understand), that she would sit on a bench crying, on the Coney Island boardwalk, because I didn't want to eat. She was a very young mother. She gave birth to me when she was seventeen-years-old.

When I was about two-years-old, my aunt and uncle bought a brand new two-family brick house on East 52nd

Street between Fillmore Avenue and Avenue S, near Flatbush Avenue, in Old Mill Basin. It was about a half hour car ride from Coney Island. My Aunt Connie and Uncle Johnny and their two daughters, Joy and Esther, moved into the upstairs apartment and my family rented the downstairs apartment. An inner staircase connected the two apartments and it connected our lives as well. All members of the family learned (me and my brother caught on as soon as we were old enough), how to hop over the wooden banisters, which crossed in an open part of the stairway, in the inside hallway of the house. Those inner staircases went from each apartment into the finished basement too. But we rarely went all the way into the basement to walk around, it was so much easier to hop over in the middle. The inner staircase was a great asset as we didn't have to go outside when it was raining, snowing, or at night. We could go upstairs or downstairs for a cup of sugar, an egg or a fried chicken cutlet and we didn't even have to get out of our pajamas. We would also go up and down with news, advice, messages and for a shoulder to cry on, if needed. It was a perfect set up for children and teens. Using the inner staircase, was the preferred way to go up and down between the apartments, but we always knocked on the inside door of the apartment, we were heading to and never just barged in.

My mother, Domenica (nicknamed Mimi) and my father, Joseph (Joey) were great, fun-loving parents.

They met on Bond St. in Carroll Gardens, Brooklyn. My brother Arthur was born soon after we moved to East 52nd Street. He was baptized in Mary Queen of Heaven Church on East 56th Street, in our new neighborhood. But I had been baptized in Sacred Hearts of Jesus and Mary-St. Stephen Church in Carroll Gardens, Brooklyn as that was the neighborhood that my parents grew up in.

My Aunt Connie, insisted that we move into the two-family house with them, on East 52nd Street. She was a very powerful, Italian woman. Aunt Connie was the matriarch of our family. She was my mother's aunt. She always looked out for my mother and was protective of her, for good reason. My maternal grandmother, Mary, (my Mom's mother who was Aunt Connie's sister), died of tuberculosis soon after my mother was born. My mother was never held in the arms of her sick mother. I often heard the sad stories of how my dying grandmother, sick with TB, couldn't touch her newborn infant, Domenica. After giving birth to my mother, she could only look at her through a glass window, separated from her infant daughter by a deadly, contagious disease. After she died, my mom as an infant, was taken to live with her grandmother and grandfather and their large family. Aunt Connie's mother, Concetta, was also a strong-willed Italian woman and she insisted on raising my mother, along with all her own children. Her thinking was that my grandfather could not care for his infant daughter, as he had to work. She also assumed my grandfather would remarry, which he did. So she told him she was taking Domenica (her newborn grand-daughter), to raise her and that he could visit whenever he wanted. It sounds strange but it wasn't uncommon at that time. After my grandfather remarried, my mother would remain close to her father and his new family but she was raised by her grandmother and grandfather and aunts and uncles. My mom always had a close bond with Aunt Connie.

That move from Coney Island to Old Mill Basin, Brooklyn when I was two-years-old was an important one, not only for me, but for my family. It was a "stepping stone" for all of us. At that time, it was similar to living in suburbia. I liked living on the ground floor of that house and having a baby brother. My bedroom window faced the backyard and I remember listening to birds singing, during the warm months and feeling secure and content in that house. My dolls liked it too! It was filled with family, friends, love and the aroma of good Italian cooking.

To grow up in the bosom of a big extended Italian family in Brooklyn, New York in the mid-1950's-'60's was an experience that is difficult to capture in words. It was pure wonder. Vibrant, life-giving, loving, exciting and stimulating are some words that come to mind to describe it. The world was changing quickly and Brooklyn was a stimulating place to be. At any stage of life, Brooklyn was (and still is) culturally, ethnically, religiously and intellectually stimulating. For a child it was lots of fun and constant excitement. It was always interesting. Life was filled with lively conversations, a variety of experiences as well as captivating personalities. It was a lot for the senses to absorb. We all thought the Old Mill Basin section of Brooklyn, was a great location. It was a couple of blocks from Flatbush Ave. and a short car ride to the beach at Riis Park on the Atlantic Ocean. It was not too far from "the city" (we called Manhattan, then and now, "the city"), a car ride to the mountains and ten minutes to the beach. It seemed like we were in the perfect spot in the Universe.

When we moved to the Old Mill Basin section of Brooklyn, that neighborhood as well as the nearby neighborhoods of Marine Park, Mill Basin, Bergen Beach and Canarsie were growing quickly. Those areas of Brooklyn had once been farms, but in the 1950's neighborhoods were being developed at a rapid rate, with new homes at affordable prices for middle-class families. My uncle drove an oil truck and my father worked for the Transit Authority and through their hard work, our families "climbed up the ladder" into the middle-class ranks in Brooklyn, alongside all the hard-working merchants, construction workers, salesmen, teachers, nurses, firemen, police officers and transit workers who lived in that part of Brooklyn.

East 52nd Street between Fillmore Ave and Ave. S was a great Brooklyn block to grow up on. It was made up of families from different ethnic and religious backgrounds, though most of the families were either Christian or Jewish. There were many churches and synagogues in that area of Brooklyn growing up and still today.

The children on the block, were all friends, regardless of our religion or background. Everyone got along. We played all those street games, famous in urban neighborhoods, like hide-n-seek, stoop ball, hit the penny, punch ball and tag. There were endless games to play. Brooklyn was a dynamic place to live. It still is. It's no wonder young people from all over the United States (and the world) move to New York City. Its cultural riches are vast and stimulating. It's a creative place and people get along for the most part and that's how it's always been. In Brooklyn and Queens, you can find people from every country of the world and for the most part, everyone gets along fine, except if two people are trying to get the same parking spot! Parking spots are a premium in New York City.

In light of the experiences I've had, I've reflected on my childhood, on the experiences I had growing up. Was there anything unusual about my upbringing? I don't think so. Was there anything that happened in my childhood that would have made me receptive to having a mystical experience later on? Yes, two events in particular. One event was a deeply meaningful, highly symbolic religious ritual/ceremony that took place when I was an infant. I was baptized into the Catholic Church, a month after I was born. In Sacred Hearts of Jesus and Mary-St. Stephen Church in Carroll Gardens, Brooklyn, my soul was flooded with grace, during the baptismal rite. (According to Church doctrine, the Sacrament of Baptism also removes the "stain" of original sin.) Years later when I was about eleven-years- old, I was confirmed. Baptism and Confirmation are two powerful sacraments of the Church, more grace-filled and powerful than most people realize. Those sacraments would have opened me to the power of the Holy Spirit and given me enough grace for the miraculous to occur. Catholics are taught and believe that we are baptized into the divine life of the Trinity. And so I was equipped for the miraculous, but not just me. All baptized, confirmed Christians are fully equipped and anointed through the graces bestowed through those sacred sacraments. Sacraments are vehicles of God's grace. Most Catholics don't fully understand how much supernatural, sanctifying grace is imparted through those sacraments, but they are both Divine anointings. (As told in the *Hebrew Scriptures*, in the world of the ancient Israelites, only priests, prophets and kings were anointed with sacred oil.) Catholics believe that through Baptism they are, "integrated into the People of God and made sharers in their particular way in the priestly, prophetic and kingly office of Christ..." (see *Catechism #897*).

Sacramental grace, infused into the soul by God, makes the extraordinary possible. As I learned through experience, it can even make the supernatural possible. Sacraments, instituted by Christ, dispense God's mercy, grace and love in abundance. Sacraments are perfect gifts from God, which bring God's presence and grace to us and within us.

In addition, there was another sacrament, which I could receive regularly, after I received my First Holy Communion, that of course was Eucharist. Going to Church and receiving Holy Communion at Sunday Mass, and hearing Scripture proclaimed, provided spiritual food and nourishment for my soul and would open me to tremendous grace and unite my soul with Jesus.

The liturgy drew me in and I knew even as a child that something very mysterious, holy and sacred was happening. During the Mass I was witnessing and experiencing on some spiritual level, the feast of the heavenly banquet, the uniting of heaven and earth. Mystically, I was praying with Christ and through Him, along with the Communion of Saints and choirs of angels, giving glory to God the Father. It was a feast for my heart, mind and soul. It calmed me and elevated me. I was awe-inspired and drew closer to the Divine through the good liturgy I experienced as a child in a Brooklyn church. It felt very good to me.

I was receptive as well. I was open to the movement of the Spirit in my life. With childlike innocence, I felt a special connectedness to God. It was a feeling I had, especially when I was in Church. I responded to the connectedness I felt to God, with love. I grew up in a large, loving family and so responding with love came natural to me. Perhaps it was a gift that I could "feel" a connectedness and closeness to God and respond as I did.

My brother who was about three years younger than me was the only male child in the house on East 52nd Street and so he was spoiled. He was a cute and chubby baby and we all adored him. I was the older sister and I loved him dearly. He was very smart and had wit and charm which was nurtured in that house, which was always filled with laughter and interesting people from all over Brooklyn who dropped by, to chat, to laugh and to eat. One famous visitor was Joe Pepitone, who played Major League Baseball for the New York Yankees. He was a friend of Joy's boyfriend. He would often drop by for some delicious Italian food, good conversation and fun times. The good food and laughter was a big draw.

With all the stimulation in that house on 52nd Street and the good schools in the area, my brother, Arthur, would grow up to be studious and competitive. He received a full scholarship from Columbia University and went on to graduate from Cornell Medical School. Eventually, he became a forensic psychiatrist. The entire family was very proud of his accomplishments. It was a big deal in our family that Arthur became a medical doctor. Unfortunately, Arthur would die at the young age of 42, from melanoma cancer. Ironically, Arthur died on the same day that Princess Diana tragically died on August 31st,1997. It seemed like I was mourning with the whole world. His loss made me realize how important my faith was to me and drew me closer to God, as my belief in God and the sacraments helped me to heal. Also, my parish faith community, comforted me and prayed for me and that was a great help. I know the importance of belonging to a faith community, it was of vital importance in my healing process. I often wonder how people without faith survive the death of a loved one or any crisis. For me, my deep faith lifted me out of my despair, over time. Arthur was a psychiatrist, so when he died I lost my brother, my friend and my therapist all at once. I was devastated and that's putting it mildly. It took me a long time to get over his premature death, but my faith in God helped and gave me courage.

My mother and father met on Bond Street in downtown Brooklyn. They fell in love and married. They had a "football wedding," an Italian-American tradition, at that time, among working-class Italians. A "football wedding," was an informal wedding reception, usually held in a neighborhood party room or hall, after Church. I heard it was great fun.

I have many memories from my childhood of visiting my father's family who lived in a brownstone in

Carroll Gardens (which was called Red Hook back then). The neighborhood has changed much to my aunts' dismay. My father's two sisters, my Aunt Margie and Aunt Alice, have only recently moved. My aunts' lamented that the Italian neighborhood they once knew, had changed so drastically through gentrification. Over the years young professionals have moved in, renovated brownstones and changed the character of the neighborhood. The Carroll Gardens they knew from their childhood and adulthood is gone and so are most of the people they knew. When I would call them to see how they were doing, they'd say to me, "Nancy Jo, we would walk down Court Street and know everyone. It would take us an hour to go a few blocks, as we would stop and talk to everybody. Now we only know a few people to say hello to, everything's changed, everyone's moved away, even the stores have different owners." My aunts worked for many years, in the nearby Catholic Church, "Our Lady Star of the Sea," and retired a few years ago. Their small corner supermarket has become a bank. Even shopping for a few items was a constant reminder of what they had and lost. Coffee shops, restaurants and outdoor cafes have sprung up in the now trendy neighborhood. Things change and there's no way to stop change. Brooklyn neighborhoods are desirable for many reasons, most of all they are only a quick train ride to and from Manhattan and from many stimulating neighborhoods, in the boroughs. Each Brooklyn neighborhood has a unique character, with cultural diversity and great ethnic food, which appeals to young professionals as well as immigrants. My grandfather bought the brownstone (that my aunts lived in), in the 1920's for $17,000, soon after he came to America from Italy. He worked long hours as a painter which enabled him to buy a brownstone in America, fulfilling the American dream. It was a home we visited often when I was a child. My grandfather, Felice and my grandmother, Nancy were good people, nurturing their family and working hard to make it in America. Looking back I can appreciate that my grandfather, my own father and all our uncles worked hard to make sure that the entire extended family "climbed the ladder" and moved into the middle-class in America. Succeeding generations have all done well, because of those hard working men, who lifted us up and gave our families opportunities as Italian-Americans, by going to work, buying houses and enabling our generation and the generations that followed to live the American dream. They helped all of us capitalize on the vast opportunities that are offered in America, then and now. Of course, the women did their part and did it well. They were also hard-working and made sure the children were nurtured, well fed, cared for, did their homework and were raised with positive Christian values and love. There were also very good schools in Brooklyn, which provided the educational foundation for children to rise into the middle-class and into the coveted upper middle-class.

There were strong parishes and good Catholic schools in Brooklyn neighborhoods as well. In the 1950's and 1960's if you were Catholic and lived in the city, people didn't ask you which neighborhood you were from, instead they asked what parish you belonged to. Our parish was Mary Queen of Heaven Parish on East 56th Street. That was the parish where I received my First Holy Communion and my Confirmation. That Church was instrumental in my religious formation. I went to catechism classes there, along with my brother and we memorized the *Baltimore Catechism* in the classrooms in the Catholic school, along with the other children in the neighborhood.

In that Church, I sensed the sacredness and holiness that was present. It enabled me to connect with the mystery and presence of God, which was real for me. Being in Church, even as a child, was comforting for me and at the same time, I was deeply moved by the religious images, paintings, statues, the stain glass and the sanctuary. It appealed to my senses, all of it. I absorbed it and felt it was very good. I was drawn to the sacredness and the religious, it felt right to me. I liked going to Mass. During part of my childhood, the Mass was still in Latin and it was very mysterious to me and drew me in. I was intrigued by the ritual actions and the sense of the sacredness that I felt. It awakened a sense of the holy within me. The Latin Mass captivated my religious sensibilities and gave me a sense and an appreciation for deep mystery, yet I remember when the changes of Vatican II were instituted, I could participate more and understand a lot more as well, so I thought those changes were good.

Growing up in a large Italian-American household, was not only nurturing but it was a feast for the mind and the body as well. My Aunt Connie was an excellent cook, as was my mother. There was always delicious food in that house on E. 52nd Street. There were also plenty of people to eat it. Joy and Esther, who were older and lived upstairs from us, had many friends (they were both popular), who visited often, day and night. Both families had friends and relatives from other parts of Brooklyn who visited as well and we had great friendships with many of our neighbors. The food that was served to our family and guests was mouth-watering: eggplant and chicken parmigiana, lasagna, stuffed peppers, rice balls, chicken spadinas, potatoes and eggs, macaroni and meatballs, stuffed artichokes and also what are known as Italian peasant dishes (pasta fagioli, beans and escarole, chick peas and rice). We were told as children that Italian-Americans ate peasant dishes during the Great Depression since they were inexpensive, nutritious and delicious. Italian families continued to eat them, even when economic times improved. Macaroni with homemade tomato sauce could be stretched so it was cooked often, in case people dropped by, there was always enough food. Traditionally, in Italian homes, if someone stopped by at mealtime, you fed them. That is why peasant dishes and pasta were an important component of meals, they could feed a lot of people and unexpected guests. When I was older and going to college, a psychology professor said in Psychology 1 that, "food is love." I knew that was true from personal experience, from growing up in an extended Italian-American household.

All of these experiences helped to form me. As I mentioned I had a natural attraction to religious things and to the Mass. I nurtured my relationship with God and would talk to God as a friend. There was never any fear. I was taught openness, receptivity, generosity, and kindness in that house on East 52nd Street. I was taught about the depths of giving, love and sacrifice, through words but more importantly through the actions of my family. For example, one winter there was a bad snowstorm. The mailman who had been drudging through the snow to deliver the mail was invited into our house for pancakes and coffee. Attention was paid to preparing and serving good food and that showed care and concern for us but also for others. There were many other stories, of people being helped and cared for, especially those down on their luck. Good Christian virtues were lived out and those positive virtues would enable me to be open to God, to open my heart freely without reservation and to value compassion and generosity throughout my life.

There was a lot of socializing, laughter, visitors and fun times in the house on E. 52nd Street. Both my parents liked to play cards, so there were some great card games in our house and elsewhere on the block too. They were serious games, so children were allowed to say hello and then had to leave to go elsewhere to play or retreat into the bedroom, at night, to go to sleep. I knew there were Catholic families, in our neighborhood who sat around the kitchen table and recited the Rosary, in the evening, but that didn't happen in our house. Nor did my parents go to Church each week. But we always went on Christmas and Easter and we observed the Lenten fast and abstinence rules. On Ash Wednesday, everyone got ashes, that was a given. But Christianity was lived out in other ways, in concrete ways, that helped me to grow up with Christian values. I was drawn to Church, the Mass and to religious objects and so I went forward, towards God, alone. I went to Church alone, when I was old enough to walk there. Sometimes my friends would come along, other times I went myself. Sometimes when I was walking to Church, mid-way to Mary Queen of Heaven Church, my father would pick me up and drive me the rest of the way. My parents never understood my desire to go to Church, they said I took after my Aunt Alice, who worked in the church in Carroll Gardens and was a trustee of the parish. But it wasn't that, it was what I felt inside that I was responding to.

My Aunt Mary and Uncle Frankie would visit often from Bensonhurst, Brooklyn. They were newly married and they enjoyed the good times on 52nd Street too. Sometimes my aunt would take me out to the movies. I remember clearly the day she picked me up and brought me to see the movie Ben-Hur. I was very impressed with that movie and it left a lasting impression on me. My aunt would also bring me gifts for special occasions. As a young child she bought me a birthday gift that would change my life. It was a colorful, illustrated Children's Bible. I still have it and cherish it to this day. Each night my mother would read me a Bible story and that started me on a faith journey and a love of Scripture. Even as a young child those biblical stories from the *Hebrew* and *Christian Scriptures* fascinated me. They captured my religious imagination. These were biblical figures who seemed real to me, they struggled with answering God's call, they were not always perfect but they tried to please God and be acceptable to God. There were exceptions, those who disobeyed God and they suffered the consequences. I was intrigued by salvation history and the concept of God. Those intriguing stories opened a world of faith and belief for me, that kept expanding and deepening as I grew older. Parents are the primary religious educators of their children and my parents taught me to say bedtime prayers and read me Bible stories. I had a long list of people I prayed for. And as a young child I was also very concerned with the welfare of my dolls, who slept at the edge of my bed. Praying came natural to me. God was always approachable. I felt close to God and prayer made that possible. I started nurturing my prayer life from an early age and I believe the Children's Bible that was a gift from my Aunt Mary and the prayers I was taught as a preschooler were the start of a deep faith that just kept growing, because I nurtured it. I felt God's presence within me and around me.

Through catechism classes at Mary Queen of Heaven Church my faith grew deeper as I began to understand more and the knowledge appealed to my rational mind and intellect. I knew instinctively it was the truth. But amazingly, I could also feel being in a special relationship with God. I now see that was a great gift. As a child, with childlike innocence, I was receptive and open to the promptings of the Holy Spirit. I could feel God's love and movement towards my soul and I responded with love and gratitude. Self-surrender came naturally, it was a child-like response.

As I've written, something about being in Church gave me a sense of peace, comfort and security. It still does. I was always focused on prayer and my relationship with God. Throughout my life, I've tried to keep focused on Jesus, especially during uncertain times and the ups and downs of life.

Aside from wanting to attend Mass and being captivated with biblical stories, the only thing that might have been unusual (but I had nothing to compare it to) was I had a deep love for God. That was just a part of who I was. I felt connected to God when I prayed. I was sure God was listening to me. I never questioned that. I had a strong sense of God in that Church and I responded with love. God initiates and we respond. As St. John wrote: *We love because God first loved us (1 John 4:19)*. Well that must be true because in a child-like way, I felt loved and I responded with love. It was simple but effective.

And so my relationship with God grew, in the midst of everything else that was going on in my childhood and teen years. All this put me on a deepening path towards God. I wouldn't find out until many years later, that some aspects of my religious journey would be unusual.

I have many memories of my childhood. Some were very funny, others very sad. Growing up in the late 1950's and the '60's was an amazing time to be alive. There were great historical movements, changes and events taking place in America such as: the Civil Rights Movement, the Feminist Movement, the Anti-War Movement, the Vietnam War, the Cold War, the Cuban Missile Crisis, which greatly affected my generation. There were devastating and senseless assassinations. I lived through the tragic assassinations of President John F. Kennedy, Dr. Martin Luther King Jr. and Senator

Bobby Kennedy. They were tumultuous times. I remember the day Apollo 11 landed on the moon. It was a big deal in Brooklyn and everywhere else. The day my family got the first color TV on the block was exciting too. Everyone crowded around it to see what the big deal was about. It was big deal for me and my brother. Many years ago, I was talking to a young woman in a gym. When I told her that I lived through the 1960's, her eyes opened wide and she said, "Wow, how cool, you lived during the '60's!" It made me think about the decades I've lived through. I've lived through historic, important times and events and I watched them unfold on television. Like other baby boomers, I've witnessed many changes in the past decades but nothing quite compares to the influence that modern technology is having on people, their lives and world events. The world is now in uncharted territory because of rapidly changing, modern technological advances.

When I was about ten-years-old my Cousin Connie, who was only a few months older than me, moved into our house, along with her older brother John and their father, Uncle Tony. There was a finished basement, with a door to the backyard, which sufficed for father and son. Cousin Connie shared a bedroom with Esther and Joy upstairs. The circumstances were tragic that caused that to happen. Uncle Tony's wife died of cancer and my Aunt Connie insisted they come live with us. She wanted her brother Tony and his children to live in our two-family house where we could nurture them, feed them (of course) and help them get over their devastating loss. The schools in our neighborhood were also very good. So the two-family house became a three-family house and naturally that brought changes with it.

I loved books as a child and as a teenager as well, but I also realized early on that experiences could be like reading chapters in a book, only they unfolded in real time. So I observed, experienced, laughed, and grew into a teenager, with my Cousin Connie alongside me. She convinced me that experiences were valuable (and fun) and useful knowledge for life. Street knowledge can be as valuable as book learned knowledge especially when you spend most of your life living or working in (or near) a large, vibrant city like New York. I loved my illustrated Bible but I also loved visiting the library and escaping to other worlds and places, through reading. I was a voracious reader. I often joked with my Cousin Connie and told her that if she hadn't moved in with us, when I was about 10 years old, I probably would have been a bookworm my entire life. I still love books, but what my cousin taught me was that there were experiences to be had, living in Brooklyn and she was determined to get me out of the house, get the books "out of my face" and get me into the neighborhood to explore and socialize. She introduced me to dancing. She knew every dance and how to do it perfectly as soon as it came out. As for me, by the time I learned one of the dances, it was "out" and time to learn a new one.

My Aunt Connie would often take us shopping to A & S Department Store in downtown Brooklyn. We would have to take the Flatbush Ave. bus, which was a long bus ride, since we lived at one end and downtown was at the other end, near the Brooklyn Bridge. It would be a treat for us, when my aunt would take us shopping. We didn't mind the bus ride. There was another whole world at the end of that bus line. It was different from where we lived and as we traveled from one neighborhood to another on that bus, we glimpsed how other Brooklynites were living. It was an eye opener and very interesting.

Esther and Joy who lived upstairs with my aunt and uncle were older than us. So they filled our lives with a lot of excitement too. They were always bringing over boyfriends and girlfriends and getting "made up," with new shades of make-up and going to get their hair done. We would sit wide-eyed as they teased their hair and made it look full and lavish. (Teasing hair in the 60's was its own art form. It was a big deal for girls to get the right teased look, with lots of volume!) They always had new clothes, the newest make-up, the latest hairstyles and we watched them with big, eager eyes, knowing in a few years we'd have more privileges and freedom and be doing the same. They were always having fun, going to parties, church dances, the movies, the beach and other outings. It was a great house to grow up in. There were always people around, stories being told, current events being discussed and laughter. Sometimes things got very serious and worrisome, that happened during the Cuban Missile Crisis (1962). That was a scary time in Brooklyn and everywhere else in America. I remember my father being concerned. He was very smart and well read and so when he got worried it was usually about a serious matter. All aspects of the crisis and other important news stories were discussed over dinner. I grew up with an interest in current events and politics that remains today. That came from my father's influence.

My Aunt Connie taught me about social justice and caring for the less fortunate. People were always being fed in the house on East 52nd Street. She would also help people down on their luck. Before my cousin and her family moved in with us, a friend of the family had lost his job and needed a place to stay for a while. My aunt called the family together and told us Jack would be moving in with us and living in the basement apartment for a short time, until he got back "on his feet." Years later at my aunt's 80th birthday party, I was asked to give a speech about her life and one of the things I said was, "I learned kindness and generosity in that house on E. 52nd Street from Aunt Connie. She helped people who were down and out and she lived her Christian faith by helping others." It was something I tried to emulate ʳ whole life, by giving of myself and helping otherʳ taught me that lesson in a very real and concrᵉ

During my early teenage years, one Sunday at Mass, a strange announcement was made by the pastor of Mary Queen of Heaven Church. A new Catholic church was being built nearby and some of the parishioners from Mary Queen of Heaven Church (and some of the other neighboring parishes) would be moving to the new church, if they lived within certain boundaries, which I did. And so like embarking on an adventure, I followed the instructions of the pastor. The new church wasn't built yet, so I wondered where Sunday Mass would be held. It turned out, until the new church was built, Sunday Masses would be held in a local nightclub, the Dorian, on Flatbush Ave. You can't make this stuff up! The founding pastor of the new church was Msgr. Edward Jolley. The church would be named St. Columba. I was fourteen years old, but I remember that I was impressed with Msgr. Jolley right away. Anyone who could pull off saying Mass in a nightclub seemed OK to me. And of course attending Mass in a nightclub was cool, unusual and intriguing all at the same time. But it worked because everyone liked Msgr. Jolley and had faith in him and his vision for the future Church of St. Columba, in Marine Park. (Msgr. Jolley served as pastor of St. Columba from 1967-88). His good homilies were instrumental in my religious formation.

When I was about fifteen, my parents told me and my brother that they had good news. The news stunned us. Even though we knew we had outgrown our apartment on East 52nd Street, we never cared about its size. The thought of moving never crossed our mind. Our parents felt it was time we had more space, a home of our own. We were moving. We were devastated at first, until we found out we were only moving a few miles away. We could visit often and still keep our same friends and stay in the same schools. But still it was quite traumatic. My aunt wasn't too happy when my parents told her that they had found a house in Marine Park, an adjoining neighborhood. Were we really moving? When something special is ending, you always know. There are certain events and experiences in life that just can't be duplicated.... ever. That was one of them and we had a sense of that. No house, no block would ever be the same. The house my family moved into was very nice, we had a dining room and a living room with a fireplace. It was much roomier than the apartment (and Arthur had a quiet space to study), but it couldn't compare to the togetherness we experienced on E. 52nd Street. Even when I married and my husband and I bought a house, also in Marine Park, it always seemed so quiet, so uneventful compared to living on E. 52nd Street. That house on E. 52nd Street was filled with family, love, constant attention, friends and neighbors flowing in and out, from all over Brooklyn, bringing news, stories, cakes, pastries and bread. Food flowed in and out of that house. It was alive and no house will ever be that alive again.

Whenever I'm in that part of Brooklyn, I drive down the block and try to remember all the good times, the memories of a time long ago. Some of it had to do with the time we lived in. It was a very different world then. There were no computers, cordless phones, cell phones, video games, Facebook, Twitter, Instagram or e-mails. But life was never dull. We had street games to keep us busy, friendships that nurtured us, traditions and family cohesiveness. It was all priceless. Looking back I realize that living in that two-family house, with a close-knit Italian family, in the middle-class neighborhood of Old Mill Basin, Brooklyn, in the time we did, was a great gift.

Your soul is called to raise itself to God by the elevator of love not to climb the rough stairway of fear. (St. Therese of Liseiux-Saint and Doctor of the Church)

Mental Prayer is nothing else than an intimate sharing between friends. It means taking time frequently to be alone with God, who we know loves us.....The important thing is not to think much but to love much and do that which best stirs you to love. (St. Teresa of Avila-Saint and Doctor of the Church)

Prayer is the best armor we have, it is the key which opens the heart of God. (St. Padre Pio)

Thus the Lord passed before Moses and cried out, 'The Lord, the Lord, a merciful and gracious God, slow to anger and rich in kindness and fidelity, continuing his kindness for a thousand generations and forgiving wickedness and crime and sin.' (Exodus 34:6-7a)

CHAPTER 2

THE MYSTICAL AND THE NOT-SO-MYSTICAL SAINTS

The model for all saints in the Church (those who have been officially canonized and all others striving to be saint-like) are the life, words and actions of Jesus Christ. Jesus said: *I am the Way, the Truth and the Life (John 14:16)*. Christian saints try to imitate Jesus and live according to His teachings. Jesus showed us what holiness truly is and how doing God's will and trusting God, at all times, is the sure path to peace, fulfillment, Heaven and glory. Jesus showed compassion, love, understanding, forgiveness and mercy to all those he came in contact with. We are called to imitate His goodness and non-judgmental attitude.

The saints continually strived for holiness of life even when challenged, gossiped about, or persecuted. Saints suffer many trials but hold fast to their faith and trust in God. They keep focused on Jesus and stay faithful to prayer, no matter what adverse circumstances arise in their lives, or in the life of the Church. They never give up hope. They never stop trusting or loving God.

Not all canonized saints are considered mystics, in the strict sense. Mystics are more likely to experience unusual mystical or religious experiences. Mystical saints have been known to experience extraordinary mystical phenomena such as: visions, locutions, bi-location, the stigmata, reading of hearts and souls, ecstasies, levitation, spiritual marriage and knowledge of divine truths.

All Christians are mystics in the broader sense, in that they have been baptized into the Paschal Mystery- the suffering, death and resurrection of Jesus and they have the divine life within them. Christians believe when they are receptive and open to God and stay connected to God through prayer, the Holy Spirit guides, comforts and helps them. Christians, throughout the world, continually witness to the power of the Holy Spirit in their lives and express how the Spirit has guided and empowered them. That is an example of mysticism in the broader sense and that is a path available to all Christians.

Catholics believe that when they receive the Body and Blood of Jesus during Holy Communion, at Mass, they partake of a divine meal. It is a deep, meaningful and sacramental communion with God that heals, transforms and calls them to continual conversion of heart and mind. Holy Communion unites them to Christ, in a mystical way. According to the Second Vatican Council: *For the most holy Eucharist contains the Church's entire spiritual wealth: Christ himself, our Passover and living bread.*

Catholics encounter the risen Christ at Mass through the living Word of God (the Scriptures) and by receiving the real presence of Jesus in the Body and Blood. The hosts and wine are transformed during the Consecration at Mass into the real presence of Jesus. Many Eucharistic miracles have confirmed the supernatural transformation of ordinary bread and wine into the Body and Blood of Christ. The risen Christ is also present in the person of the priest and in the power of the sacrament. Catholics are called to respond with prayer, gratitude, awe, praise to God and conversion of heart. With Christ, we give praise and glory to God the Father at Mass. This encounter with Christ is mystical, in every sense of the word and should be experienced as a mystical encounter with the Risen Christ. There are many accounts of mystical saints who have experienced ecstasy after receiving Holy Communion, such as St. Catherine of Siena, St. Teresa of Avila and the Venerable Fr. Solanus Casey.

Jesus said to them, 'Amen, Amen, I say to you, unless you eat the flesh of the Son of Man and drink his blood, you do not have life within you. Whoever eats my flesh and drinks my blood has eternal life and I will raise him on the last day. For my flesh is true food and my blood is true drink. Whoever eats my flesh and drinks my blood remains in me and I in him' (John 6:53-56).

'I am the vine, you are the branches. Whoever remains in me and I in him will bear much fruit, because without me you can do nothing' (John 15:5).

Saints truly understand that being united to Christ, through prayer and the sacraments is the way to fulfillment, holiness and wholeness and gives glory to God the Father.

All saints are in love with God and try to fulfill the call they have received from God, that is very real for them. Denying Christ or Christ's call is unthinkable for them.

The early Catholic saints were martyrs. They willingly gave their life for Christ and "The Way." They refused to deny Christ, knowing they would die for their beliefs. Those ancient saints were honored as saints by public acclaim. One heroic story, among many, is the amazing story of the famous martyrs from Carthage- Saints Perpetua and Felicity. Their strong belief in Christ and the heroism they showed, was so inspiring to the early Christians that their story (Perpetua's prison diary) was read during or after liturgies in the early centuries of the Church. Their account is known as: *The Martyrdom of Perpetua and Felicity.* Perpetua was a noblewoman who was nursing her infant son at the time of her arrest. Her father begged her to deny Christ, to save her life and for the sake of her son. Her father was filled with grief over her decision. She wrote: *It shall happen as God shall choose, for assuredly we depend not on our own power but on the power of God.* Felicity, who was pregnant when she was imprisoned, was a slave. She gave birth to her daughter, before she was martyred. Both Perpetua and Felicity, as well as other Christians died a horrible death, in the Roman amphitheater at the public games. Both Perpetua and Felicity were beheaded while other Christians were killed by wild animals. Their bravery in refusing to deny Christ inspired Christians, throughout the Roman Empire and beyond, to stand up for their beliefs, even in the face of ridicule, persecution and death. It is believed they were martyred in A.D. 203 in a Roman Province of Africa (modern day Tunisia).

Sadly, there are still Christian martyrs in the modern world, who are giving their lives for the gospel and for belief in Jesus Christ. They come up against evil and fearlessly stand up for truth. In the last one hundred years, millions have been martyred for their faith. It seems every week there is an alarming news story of another religious sister or brother, priest, or missionary being martyred for their faith in Christ. The horrific killing of an eighty-five year old French priest, Father Jacques Hamel on July 26,[th]2016 while celebrating Mass at his parish outside Rouen, sickened all decent people of the world. He was killed by two extremists. A couple of months later, on September 14th, Pope Francis declared him a "martyr" and "blessed." The Pope reminded the faithful in his homily that: *Jesus Christ was the first martyr, the first who gave his life for us...... From this mystery of Christ begins the whole history of Christian martyrdom, from the first centuries to this day...Fr. Jacques is a part of that chain of Christian martyrs.*

Saints come from all walks of life. Some were peasants or slaves, others were from nobility. Some saints, challenged by the gospel message, focused their lives on helping the poor, like St. Teresa of Calcutta (1910-1997). Sister Teresa was a Roman Catholic nun from Albania, whose missionary work brought her to Calcutta. While in India, she received from God what she described as, "a call within a call." Three mystical visions followed in the months ahead which validated the "call" for her. According to her personal account, on September 10th, 1946 while she was traveling by train from Calcutta to the Loreto Convent in Darjeeling, India for a religious retreat, she felt compelled by God's call to leave her comfortable and rewarding teaching job in Calcutta to go out into the slums, to work with the poor. She said of the religious experience: *I was to leave the convent and help the poor, while being among them. It was an order. To fail would have been to break the faith.* At first no one, most especially her Mother Superior, nor her students or the local bishop could understand Mother Teresa's special "call." She persevered and moved forward to fulfill God's will and be obedient to God's call on her life. In 1948, she began her missionary work in the slums, exchanging her traditional religious habit for a simple white sari, trimmed with a blue border. Soon people began to see the "fruit" of her long hours of prayer, hard work in the slums and her dedication to the call she received from God. People began to help her. She continued her work among the poor, focused on Christ, even though for many years, she experienced a "dark night of the soul." She described in conversation and letters to her spiritual director of feeling desolation, loneliness and "darkness" in prayer. In one letter, to the Rev. Michael van der Peet, she wrote: *The silence and the emptiness is so great, that I look and do not see, listen and do not hear.* Yet, regardless of the "emptiness" and the sense of the absence of God, she inwardly felt in prayer, she continued to dedicate all her energy and life's work to the "poorest of the poor," and to the religious order she founded in 1950-The Missionaries of Charity. She was known as the "saint of the gutters," for her selfless work with lepers, the abandoned, the unloved and the dying. She gave dignity to the dying by caring for each one, as if they were Christ. She gained respect and was honored during her lifetime, for her selfless work and for inspiring others to join her in her noble work in India and throughout the world. She received the Nobel Peace Prize in 1979. At the acceptance lecture in Oslo, she said: *It is not enough for us to say, 'I love God but I do not love my neighbor,' since in dying on the Cross, God had made himself the hungry one, the naked one, the homeless one........Jesus' hunger is what you and I must find and alleviate.* She met and was photographed with celebrities, politicians, royalty and famous people from all walks of life. People wanted to be near a living saint and they were not disappointed. Many of those who met her said that when she looked into your eyes, or held your hand, it was a deeply moving spiritual experience. That is often said about saints.

There were some who criticized her but their voices were drowned out by her good works. She visited New York City many times. As a native New Yorker, I eagerly watched the television news programs and segments devoted to her visits and read articles in the New York City newspapers. This inspiring, influential saint lived during my lifetime and she made a difference in my life as well. In 1981, Mayor Ed Koch gave her a key to the city. In 1997, I remember seeing a beautiful photograph of her that was printed in newspapers, around the world. She was holding hands with Princess Diana, which was very touching. The beautiful Princess Diana visited the Bronx Mission of the Missionaries of Charity, with Mother Teresa at her side. They were both extraordinary women. As humanitarians, they tried, each in their own unique way, to help the less fortunate among us. Their celebrity status enabled them to bring needed attention to the most vulnerable and causes important to them. They each had a special gift of connecting to people. Sadly, that meeting in the Bronx, would be the last time Princess Di and Mother Teresa would see each other, in this world. Within three months, they would both die. Yet their noble work continues through the efforts of those who admired and loved them.

Mother Teresa had single-minded focus on Christ and the poor. She brought Christ's healing touch to all those she met and the mercy of God was made manifest in her encounters with the poor and destitute. She was quoted as saying: *I never think in terms of crowds, but in terms of persons. Were I to think about crowds, I would never begin anything. It is the person that matters. I believe in person-to-person encounters.* That was obvious to the entire Missionary of Charity family, to all the volunteers who helped, to those who visited with them and those who were cared for. She died at the age of 87, at the convent in Calcutta. According to her nuns, who were at her deathbed, her last words were: *Jesus, I love you.* Two confirmed miracles occurred after her death, including the miraculous healing of a Brazilian man, who was healed from multiple brain tumors, thus paving the way for her canonization.

On September 4th, 2016 on a sunny, beautiful day in St. Peter's Square, in the presence of a massive crowd of international pilgrims, which included thousands of religious, she was canonized by Pope Francis and added to the Canon of Saints. Among those who cheered at the canonization Mass were nuns, brothers, priests and lay members of the Missionaries of Charity family. The Pope said at the canonization Mass that Mother Teresa was a *dispenser of Divine Mercy*. She showed the world Christ's love, compassion and mercy in a concrete way, in the modern world. Her work continues. The Missionaries of Charity family (which now includes a lay order-the Lay Missionaries of Charity) are active in 139 countries throughout the world and have 130 houses serving the poor. Her influence, through her congregation and intercession from Heaven continues after her death. According to news reports, over 1,700 parishes have already requested relics of St. Teresa of Calcutta and I'm sure that number will continue to grow.

There are countless saints who founded religious orders, hospitals, started Catholic schools and educational programs and worked with the marginalized. They have worked with young people, the elderly, the homeless, prisoners or spent their lives in the missions, making great sacrifices. There are canonized saints who were: popes, bishops, priests, nuns, monks, scholars, soldiers, lawyers, teachers, queens, noblemen and noblewomen. Others have been humble and unassuming laypeople or religious. Some were married, others were single. Some belonged to Third Orders, like St. Catherine of Siena, who was a Third Order Dominican. Some were stern and serious, while others could easily laugh at themselves and others. In every time period, saintly people have made a positive difference in the world as they've tried to put flesh-and-blood, on Christ's call to serve and give witness to the gospel message.

The autobiographies as well as biographies of the saints have always fascinated me. I believe, as others do, that saints are some of the most interesting and generous people who have ever lived. Their stories are worth reading and have inspired many people to seek conversion and holiness of life.

St. Francis of Assisi, the founder of the Franciscan Order was born in Assisi, Italy in 1181. He is considered the most popular and beloved of all the saints. He is the patron saint of animals and ecology and the co-patron of Italy. His religious experience in the Church of San Damiano is legendary. According to his account, as he was praying before the ancient icon crucifix, he heard the voice of Christ, three times, exhorting him: "Go Francis and repair my house, which as you see is falling into ruin." Shaken to the core, Francis took the command literally and began to repair the old church. In time, he came to realize that Christ was calling him to help renew and revitalize the Catholic Church.

St. Katherine Drexel (1858-1955) of Philadelphia is a canonized saint I greatly admire. She was an heiress and philanthropist, who became a nun and foundress of a religious congregation- the Sisters of the Blessed Sacrament. Her father, Francis Anthony Drexel was an investment banker and when he died she inherited considerable wealth, along with her sisters. Her interest in helping Native Americans came from a family trip out West in 1884. The plight of American Indians haunted her and she became interested in helping them. Eventually she gave her considerable wealth away, to help African-Americans and American Indians, giving her life to Christ and the poor and never looking back. She was ahead of her time. She took to heart Jesus' challenge: *Amen, I say to you, whatever you did for one of these least brothers of mine, you did for me (Matthew 25:40).*

A famous story is told about the conversion of St. Ignatius of Loyola (1491-1556), the founder of the Society of Jesus (the Jesuits), and its first Superior General. He was born into a wealthy Basque, Catholic family, in northeastern Spain, in the 15th century. His birth took place in the ancestral castle of the Loyola family. Both his parents came from noble and illustrious lineage. However, his father and grandfather were on the wild side. His mother died when he was very young. He was the youngest of thirteen children and was raised to be a courtier and a diplomat. Later in life he became a knight in the Spanish army. He was known for his bravery and respected even by his enemies. While fighting in the Battle of Pamplona, against the French, he was wounded by a cannonball. During his long recovery, he was given a book on the lives of the saints as well as an illustrated copy of *De Vita Christi (Life of Christ)*. Both books greatly influenced him and his conversion began. During his convalescence, he began to think about how he could imitate St. Francis of Assisi and St. Dominic and thus began his life-changing encounter with Christ, who took hold of St. Ignatius and never let go. During that time, he had a vision of the Blessed Mother holding the Holy Child Jesus and afterwards made a pilgrimage to her shrine in Montserrat, in the mountains above Barcelona. He left his sword and dagger there, leaving behind his old life of flamboyance and recklessness, for a life devoted to Christ. At nearby Manresa, where he remained for almost a year, praying for long hours at a time, (sometimes in a cave), he began his greatest work, "The Spiritual Exercises." All his actions, work and writings were for the "greater glory of God." His life produced great "fruit" for his religious order as well as the Church. Pope Francis is the most famous modern day Jesuit. St. Ignatius must be proud that the religious order he founded has produced a much loved and respected Pope of the modern age! One can imagine St. Ignatius brimming with pride in Heaven.

St. Edith Stein was born in 1891 in Breslau, Germany into an observant Jewish family. She would die a horrible death, in a gas chamber in Auschwitz in 1942, (along with her sister Rosa). During her lifetime, she achieved recognition as a brilliant German philosopher. She was a teaching assistant to Edmund Husserl and received a doctorate degree in 1917 after writing a thesis titled: "The Problem of Empathy." Eventually she converted to Catholicism after witnessing the strong faith of her Christian friends and being influenced by the writings of saints. While visiting a Christian friend whose husband had recently died, she experienced the healing power of faith in God. She later wrote: *This was my first encounter with the Cross and the divine power it imparts to those who bear it...it was the moment when my unbelief collapsed and Christ began to shine his light on me-Christ in the mystery of the Cross.* She was also very impressed and influenced after reading the autobiography of St. Teresa of Avila. While staying at a friend's house, she stayed up all night reading St. Teresa's autobiography, "Life" and in the morning exclaimed: *This is the truth!* After converting to Catholicism, she became a Discalced Carmelite nun, taking as her religious name, Teresa Benedicta of the Cross (Teresa Blessed by the Cross). She wrote: *My longing for truth was a single prayer.* Though she was a Catholic nun, she was not spared during the Holocaust. The Gestapo entered the Carmelite Convent in Echt, in the Netherlands on August 2nd, 1942 and arrested Sr. Teresa Benedicta and her sister, because they were Jewish Christians. (This was in retaliation against the Dutch bishops who had written a protest letter against the treatment of the Jews.) Her last words in the Convent were spoken to her sister. She was overheard saying:

Come we are going for our people. They died in Auschwitz, along with other Jewish Christians who had been arrested, at that time, because of their Jewish lineage. A tragic story.

All saints have shown heroic virtue. Their good works, heroic virtue and inspiring stories continue to bear "fruit" after their death. The miracles attributed to their intercession astound the medical profession. Their writings and the power of their stories to inspire is a great testament to the lasting power of sanctity and a life well lived.

Yet the mystical saints, who have experienced extraordinary mystical phenomena stand apart in that they have had unusual religious experiences and those experiences and their writings have proved "fruitful" in both a mystical and concrete way, for the Church. Their writings are filled with wisdom, insights, spiritual knowledge of the divine and in-depth knowledge of prayer. Many scholars believe, after studying their writings that they could not have achieved or had access to divine knowledge on their own but were inspired by God. St. Teresa of Avila, a 16th century Spanish Carmelite nun reformed the Carmelite Order (her reform led to the establishment of the Order of Discalced Carmelites, a separate order from the Order of Carmelites). She was a good friend and collaborator with another Spanish mystical saint, St. John of the Cross. He was a great mystical writer, poet and reformer. Teresa was an extraordinary woman and mystic, in her time. She founded fourteen convents throughout Spain, (though she suffered from physical ailments), was the only woman to ever reform a men's religious order, all the while keeping a very active life, a deep prayer life and experiencing unusual mystical experiences. She drew suspicion in her own day and was ridiculed, misunderstood and mocked by some, even within her own religious order. Her writings and her actions were under suspicion by the Inquisition. Yet her writings and her mystical experiences were fully investigated by the Church and eventually she was canonized a saint (1622) and later given the honorary title of Doctor of the Church (September 1970) as well as recognized as "Mater Spritualium"-Mother of Spirituality. (Both St. Teresa of Avila and St. Catherine of Siena were named the first women Doctors of the Church in 1970 by Pope Paul VI, in recognition of the influence of their spirituality and the importance of their writings for Catholics. In a ceremony, the Pope mentioned St. Teresa's *human vitality and spiritual vivacity.)*

During her lifetime, St. Teresa's confessors and spiritual directors were amazed at her knowledge (and the locutions and visions she experienced). She described to her spiritual director of having visions of Jesus in bodily form (though invisible). Teresa's insights surpassed all the knowledge and years of schooling of her spiritual directors. She had great insights into the spiritual life, prayer, theology and God, that came from her deep prayer life and her mystical experiences (she had no formal instruction in theology). Teresa believed she was taught by God. She wrote many books on prayer and is known as the Doctor of Prayer. St. Teresa felt strongly that Christians should think often of Jesus' Passion and Resurrection. She often contemplated Jesus in the Garden of Gethsemane. She wrote in her autobiography, that we should *delight in the Lord's presence.* She also wrote: *The Lord almost always showed Himself as risen and also when he appeared in the Host-except at times when He showed me His wounds in order to encourage me when I was suffering tribulation. Sometimes he appeared on the cross or in the garden and a few times with the crown of thorns; sometimes He also appeared carrying the cross on account as I say, of my needs and those of others. But his body was always glorified (Life,29,4).*

Nuns from her religious order, often observed her ecstasies and her other extraordinary mystical gifts. Witnesses described seeing her levitating during Mass.

In a dramatic vision, she described in her autobiography, "The Book of Her Life," of seeing an angel who drove the fiery point of a lance, through her heart over and over again. In her words: *I saw in his hands a large golden dart and at the end of the iron tip there appeared to be a little fire. It seemed to me this angel plunged the dart several times into my heart and that it reached deep within me. When he drew it out, I thought he was carrying off with him the deepest part of me; he left me all on fire with great love of God (Life, 29,13).*

The great Italian sculptor and architect, Gian Lorenz Bernini immortalized that description in his famous life-size, white marble statue titled, *The Ecstasy of St. Teresa* (or *Transverberation of St. Teresa*). The sculptural masterpiece is located in the Cornaro Chapel in Santa Maria della Vittoria, Rome.

St. Catherine of Siena, a Dominican laywoman (1347-1380) is also a canonized saint and a Doctor of the Church. Her mystical experiences started as a child. She recalled to others an amazing experience she had one evening in Siena, while walking home with her brother. According to her account, she glanced at the Church of San Domenico, in the distance and saw a vision of Jesus. She described him wearing gold vestments, a papal crown, while sitting on a throne. He was surrounded by St. Peter, St. Paul and St. John the Evangelist. Jesus made the Sign of the Cross.

St. Catherine had many mystical gifts and was a bold and outspoken woman in her time. Imagine getting a letter from her that began with these words: *I, Caterina, servant and slave of the servants of Jesus Christ, am writing to you in his precious blood. I long to see you clothed in the wedding garment without which I know we cannot please our Creator or have a place at the wedding feast of everlasting life…..*It seems even Pope Gregory XI took notice of her reputation for holiness and heeded her advice. She wrote him many letters and finally visited him in Avignon and spoke against the sins of the papal court. She begged him to return the papacy to Rome, and leave the palace in Avignon, France, where he was residing. (Seven French popes had resided in France.) Catherine was sure that it was God's will that the papacy return to Rome and she finally convinced him of that. She didn't mince words when writing to him or in person. These words from the *Book of Wisdom* would be fulfilled in the life of St. Catherine and other saints as well:

> *Those who trust in him shall understand truth, and the faithful shall abide with him in love: because grace and mercy are with his holy ones and his care is with his elect (Wisdom 3:9).*

Many of the mystical saints insisted that God (or in some cases Mary-the Blessed Mother), taught them and guided them to divine truths. St. Catherine was one of them. She was obedient to God's will and she expected that of others. According to her biographers, she often challenged Religious men who she thought should live more humbly. She called them to repentance and many of them changed their way of life, after being confronted with bold accusations from holy Catherine. They humbly accepted that she was speaking to them of God's will for their lives. Very impressive indeed!

For some saints, their deep love of God opened for them a mystical path, and in their writings they try to help others navigate a path that will bring them closer to God. From my studies, (and from what scholars have written) it seems the mystics didn't do anything special to open themselves to mystical experiences in the strict sense. These were unusual graces or gifts, given to certain people of faith. Why some people are chosen for supernatural mystical experiences remains a mystery. At times, God has chosen the least likely people for mystical experiences and divine revelation. For example, St. Paul, before his conversion, was a Pharisee who persecuted Christians. Jesus transformed his life by appearing to him in a blinding light. On the road to Damascus, Jesus shook Saul's existence to the core by appearing in a vision and saying to him: *Saul, Saul why are you persecuting me?* *(Acts 9:4).* Jesus identified Himself with all the Christians who were being persecuted by Saul. Saul was told to be baptized and he was then welcomed into the Church. During the events that followed and over time, Saul, whose Christian name became Paul, became one of the greatest Christian evangelizers of all time. Scholars believe that he traveled over 10,000 miles by sea and 4,000 miles by land spreading the Good News of Jesus Christ. He believed he should be recognized as an apostle. He wrote: *Have I not seen Jesus our Lord? (1 Cor. 9:1).* His authority came from Christ, as he wrote to the converts in Galatia: *Now I want you to know, brothers, that the gospel preached by me is not of human origin. For I did not receive it from a human being, nor was I taught it, but it came through a revelation of Jesus Christ. (Gal. 1:11-12).*

St. Therese of Lisieux, the Little Flower, (1873-1897), a French Carmelite nun, was declared the youngest Doctor of the Church by Pope St. John Paul II in October 1997. She is a much loved and venerated saint. (I have a deep devotion to St. Therese and have two of her relics-tiny pieces of her brown religious habit, encased in small reliquaries.) Therese only lived to 24 years of age but developed an extraordinary spirituality of the "little way" and a deep love for Jesus, in her short life. She suffered much at the end of her life and experienced a "dark night of the soul," but she continued loving Jesus, with a mystical love. Her dying words were, "My God, I love you!"

Therese entered religious life at the young age of fifteen, entering the Carmelite convent in Lisieux. She came from a very holy family. Her sisters, (Pauline, Marie, Celine and Leonie) all entered religious life. Her parents, Louis Martin and Marie-Zelie Martin were deeply religious and instilled a love of God and the Church in their daughters. (They were canonized by Pope Francis in 2015, during the same ceremony.) Therese was a spiritual genius, who desired to be a saint. She realized she would have to depend on God to lift her to heights she couldn't attain on her own. Therese wrote: *The elevator which must raise me to heaven is your arms, O Jesus! And for this I had no need to grow up, but rather I had to remain little and become this more and more.* In the convent, Therese was given responsibility for assisting with the novices. She would astound the novices with her in-depth knowledge of their thoughts and feelings. Her explanation to the novices is quite telling: *Here is my secret. I never advise you without having invoked the Blessed Virgin. I ask her to inspire me to say what will do you the most good and I myself am often surprised at the things I teach you. I only know that in speaking to you I am not mistaken, and that Jesus speaks to you through me.* Therese had a great devotion and love for the Blessed Mother, as expressed in the beautiful poem she wrote for Mary-*Why I love you, O Mary.*

Therese's autobiography: *Story of a Soul,* has been referred to as a supernatural book. It is well worth reading.

Mystical saints were often tempted and harassed by the Devil but they held their ground and survived the assaults, through prayer, confident that Jesus was at their side. In modern times, St. Padre Pio's struggles and battles with the devil and demons are well documented and very unnerving to read about. St. Catherine of Siena also described, in her writings and to her spiritual directors, her many inner battles and struggles with the devil. Many of the saints, like Jesus Himself, have accounts of fighting off temptations, the devil and evil spirits as well. St. Teresa of Avila believed in the power of holy water to ward off devils and temptations and she would use it when she felt threatened. She wrote: *I know by frequent experience that nothing puts the devils to flight like holy water.* She claimed that a devil once sat on her prayer book so she couldn't finish her prayers. St.

Teresa learned from God that she should be bold, when dealing with devils, as God was at her side and she had nothing to fear. She used holy water and confidence in God to send them fleeing.

The old monks would say: *I psalmed down the devil*, so reciting the psalms is a powerful weapon against evil and many saints have quoted the psalms and other Scripture verses when faced with threats from the devil.

In St. Paul's *Letter to the Ephesians*, he makes it clear, that all of us, have to be aware of the presence of evil in the world and stand our ground, through prayer and holy action.

> *Our struggle is not with flesh and blood but with the principalities, with the powers, with the world rulers of this present darkness, with the evil spirits in the heavens. Therefore, put on the armor of God, that you may be able to resist on the evil day and having done everything, to hold your ground (Eph. 6:12-13).*

St. Padre Pio (1887-1968) had many unusual supernatural gifts. One of them was the power to "read souls." He could look deeply into someone's soul and "see" what their sins were. Many years ago, I heard a first-hand account during a special Church program, in Brooklyn, from a devotee of Padre Pio. He told a fascinating story of meeting Padre Pio in person. He had traveled to San Giovanni Rotondo in southern Italy to wait in line for

Padre Pio to hear his Confession. He waited for over 12 hours, as Padre Pio drew great crowds to the confessional. Finally, when he sat down in the confessional, to confess his sins, Padre Pio looked at him intently and then proceeded to tell the man what he believed his sins were. Padre Pio had looked deeply into this man's soul and "saw" his sins and faults. The man sat in stunned silence. This amazing mystical gift that Padre Pio had of "reading souls" was experienced by countless believers, in the confessional. Naturally the speaker, who experienced this phenomena was deeply moved, repented of all his sins and went on to devote the rest of his life to spreading Padre Pio's message. Another unusual gift that St. Padre Pio had was the gift of bi-location. He was often seen in two different places at the same time, according to witnesses.

However, the supernatural gift which brought Padre Pio controversy as well as great fame was the stigmata. In the year 1918, he was praying in the Church of Our Lady of Grace when the wounded Christ appeared to him. When the vision ended, Padre Pio had received the stigmata, the five wounds of Christ. He would bear the stigmata for the rest of his life.

St. Faustina was an extraordinary mystic, in the strict sense. She had repeated visions of Jesus and spoke with Him. Her story is incredible. St. Faustina's visions have produced great "fruit" for the Church and the faithful, a sure sign her visions were authentic.

St. Faustina, (her birth name was Helena Kowalska) was born in 1905 in Poland and died in 1938 at the age of 33. She came from a large, poor, religious family. Before entering religious life, she worked as a nanny to help support her family. She felt the call to religious life but was discouraged initially by her parents because they didn't have the money for the dowry, which most convents required at that time. She finally was accepted to the Sisters of Our Lady of Mercy, after she earned enough money to pay for her habit. Before entering the convent, she had a vision of Jesus. She saw a vision of Christ crucified, bloodied and he questioned her, "How long are you going to make me wait?" That challenging question, confirmed her desire to become a nun.

As a nun, Sr. Faustina would receive special revelations and visions from Jesus and have conversations with him. Jesus revealed himself as, *The Divine Mercy.* Sr. Faustina wrote the 600 page *Diary* that later became a book, (*Diary of St. Maria Faustina Kowalska:Divine Mercy in My Soul),* that describes the visions and words of Jesus. The Lord said to Sr. Faustina: *Your task is to write down every thing that I make known to you about my mercy, for the benefit of those who by reading these things will be comforted in their souls and will have the courage to approach me* (*Diary,* 1693). Trusting in Jesus is the essence of the message of mercy that Sr. Faustina received. Jesus said:

I have opened my heart as a living fountain of mercy. Let all souls draw life from it. Let them approach this sea of mercy with great trust (Diary, 1520).

On the cross the fountain of my Mercy was opened wide by the lance, for souls, no one have I excluded (Diary,1182).

The graces of my mercy are drawn by means of one vessel only and that is—trust. The more a soul trusts, the more *it will receive (Diary,1578).*

Jesus said: *I am love and mercy itself. When a soul approaches me with trust I fill it with such an abundance of graces that it cannot contain them within itself, but radiates them to other souls (Diary,1074).*

On February 22, 1931, Jesus appeared to Sr. Faustina, with a most special message. In her *Diary* she explains what happened. *In the evening, when I was in my cell, I became aware of the Lord Jesus clothed in a white garment. One hand was raised in blessing, the other was touching the garment at the breast. From the opening of the garment at the breast there came forth two large rays, one red and the other pale. In silence I gazed intently at the Lord; my soul was overwhelmed with fear, but also with great joy. After a while Jesus said to me, 'paint an image according to the pattern you see, with the inscription: Jesus, I trust in You' (Diary, 47).*

The image which Sr. Faustina had painted, (since she was unable to paint it herself) according to her vision, has become the famous image of Divine Mercy, which hangs in Catholic churches, schools, and thousands of Catholic homes, throughout the world. It has been printed on holy cards, painted on wood and canvas and made into sculptures. The artist, Eugene Kazimirowski tried to paint it exactly as Sr. Faustina described, but it took twelve tries before she accepted it.

People of faith experience special graces through the Divine Mercy image as well as from the powerful but simple prayer, "Jesus I trust in you." Jesus told St. Faustina that: *Humanity will never find peace, until it turns with trust to my Divine Mercy (Diary, 132).*

Sr. Faustina was canonized by Pope St. John Paul II in the year 2000. She is venerated in the Church as the "Secretary of Divine Mercy." The Pope officially established the Feast of Divine Mercy, on the first Sunday after Easter, at that time. (Jesus told Sr. Faustina that is what He wished.) The Pope said at that Mass, in his homily:

And you Faustina, a gift from God, to our time, a gift from the land of Poland to the whole Church, obtain for us an awareness of the depth of divine mercy, help us to have a living experience of it and to bear witness to it among our brothers and sisters. May your message of light and hope spread throughout the world, spurring sinners to conversion, calming rivalries and hatred and opening individuals and nations to the practice of brotherhood. Today, fixing our gaze with you on the face of the risen Christ, let us make our own your prayer of trusting abandonment and say with firm hope: 'Christ Jesus, I trust in you!'

Saints want others to love God as they do and to give honor and glory to God. *The Great Commandment,* also called *The Law of Love-* is paramount in their lives. They call us and challenge us to love God with our whole heart, mind and soul and love others as well as ourselves.

The Great Commandment from *St. Matthew's Gospel* in the *New Testament*

When the Pharisees heard that he (Jesus) had silenced the Sadducees, they gathered together and one of them, a scholar of the law, tested him by asking, 'Teacher, which commandment in the law is the greatest?' He said to them, 'You shall love the Lord, your God, with all your heart, with all your soul and with all your mind. This is the greatest and the first commandment. The second is like it: You shall love your neighbor as yourself. The whole law and the prophets depend on these two commandments.' (Matthew 22:34-40)

**The Great Commandment from *The Book of
Deuteronomy* in the *Hebrew Scriptures***

*Hear, O Israel. The Lord is our God, the Lord
alone. Therefore, you shall love the Lord your God
with all your heart and all your soul and with all your
strength. Take to heart these words which I enjoin on
you today. Drill them into your children. Speak of them
at home and abroad, whether you are busy or at rest....
(Dt. 6:4-7)*

Behold, I stand at the door and knock. If anyone hears my voice and opens the door, then I will enter his house and dine with him, and he with me. (Revelation 3:20)

Then he touched their eyes and said, 'Let it be done for you according to your faith.' And their eyes were opened. (Mt. 9: 29-30

Hark my lover, here he comes springing across the mountains, leaping across the hills. My lover is like a gazelle or a young stag. Here he stands behind our wall, gazing through the windows, peering through the lattices. My lover speaks, he says to me, 'Arise, my beloved, my beautiful one and come!' (Song of Songs 2:8-10)

Mysticism is *"experiential knowledge of God."* (Hans Urs von Balthasar

CHAPTER 3

WHAT IS MYSTICISM? THE DIRECT EXPERIENCE OF GOD'S PRESENCE

I n the last chapter I tried to give examples of some of the mystical experiences of well known saints. I've only mentioned a few of the hundreds of holy men and women who have been officially canonized by the Church, who experienced unusual religious experiences. Before canonizing saints, who were mystics, in the strict sense, the Church had to thoroughly evaluate and investigate: their experiences and writings, the holiness they exhibited, the presence of heroic virtue in their lives, the good works they did and approved miracles attributed to their intercession. Given the unusual nature of mysticism, the Church is very careful when investigating mystical experiences, of a saintly person. It is crucial for the Congregation for the Causes of Saints, (the department of the Roman Curia that oversees the canonization process), that when they delve into the supernatural aspects of a saint's life, they handle the findings with care and prudence. Expert testimony is considered from varied sources: witnesses and relatives (when possible), observations of friends or members of religious communities, writings or interviews with spiritual directors, findings of medical doctors, theologians, church officials, cardinals, bishops and priests. The canonization process is a serious, complex and multifaceted process, which takes years to complete and happens in stages. Extensive proof is required that the deceased person being considered for sainthood lived a holy life and showed heroic virtue. The process begins at the diocesan level and the scrutiny of the person starts there. When mysticism is present in the life of a saintly person, the mystical experiences must be scrutinized, to ensure they were authentic and from God. St. Teresa of Avila wrote: *From what I see and know through experience, a locution bears the credentials of being from God, if it is in conformity with Sacred Scripture (Life,25,13).* That is true, but it even goes beyond that. Mystical experiences in any form, can never contradict or surpass Sacred Scripture, Sacred Tradition, the *Catechism of the Catholic Church* or the Magisterium-the teaching authority of the Church.

There are ordinary Catholics, who have had private revelations and mystical experiences. Some of those

Catholics, like myself, believe that they have had an authentic mystical experience, in the strict sense or what theologians refer to as extraordinary mystical phenomena. As I've mentioned in an earlier chapter, millions of Catholics, throughout the world experience mysticism in the broader sense. I am well aware of Catholics (as well as Christians from other denominations throughout the world), who at different times, claimed to have visions, which had messages, warnings, and claims attached to them. Some of them have been investigated and approved, while others have not. In some cases, Catholics have been forbidden to visit the site of the alleged apparition or take part in any prayer services or gatherings nearby. One famous case that was **not** approved by the Church, after investigation and caused quite a stir in Queens, New York and the Diocese of Brooklyn, (the diocese comprises both Brooklyn and Queens) was the so-called apparitions of Mary in Bayside, New York.

The most important thing to remember about private revelations, even when they are approved by the Church, is that Catholics are not required to believe in them or visit the shrines or pilgrimage sites. They can if they wish and many Catholics are edified by going on pilgrimages to holy sites that have been approved, but it's optional for the faithful.

Regarding the mystical experience that I will describe in this book, it happened to an ordinary Catholic, living in Brooklyn and that ordinary Catholic would be me. Though the experience didn't last long, it made a lasting impression on me. (How could it not?) The apparition of the Risen Christ, that I saw in a sanctuary of a Catholic Church in Brooklyn was silent. There were no commands, words spoken, requests or instructions. As it was, I was completely "frozen," unable to move, all my senses were totally absorbed. I think if Jesus had said one word to me, I would have fainted. I wasn't fearful because there were people in Church with me. Also, the apparition was humble, beautiful and peaceful. I was surrounded by people, who were present at the prayer meeting in the Church, though no one was directly near me. (It was usually a small group that gathered in Church on Friday evenings.) But that doesn't matter, I couldn't move, I was transfixed. I was overawed! When I hear of saints, (and that's one of the reasons they are saints!), who have had conversations with apparitions of Jesus or Mary, I'm amazed at that. I can't imagine conversing with an apparition. I would not have been able to speak, even if I wanted to. I imagine those blessed and extraordinary saints, like St. Faustina were given a special grace to converse with Jesus. I felt as if I couldn't move one muscle of my body, at the time of the vision. I was standing at the time of the experience, (along with others in Church), singing and giving praise to God at a Catholic Charismatic Prayer Group which met every Friday. Over the years when thinking about the experience, I would get upset with myself. Upon reflection, I wondered why I didn't try to kneel in the presence of the apparition. Kneeling would have been an appropriate response. Then I recall I felt as if I couldn't move, I was transfixed, so even if the thought had entered my mind to kneel, I wouldn't have been able to. But the thought of kneeling didn't enter my mind, my mind was totally absorbed with trying to focus on what I was seeing. My human mind was overloaded, it was seeing something miraculous and supernatural and it was an all encompassing experience. I realized afterwards that no one else saw what I saw, because there was no mention of anything unusual happening that evening. There was a Catholic priest in the Church at the time, as was usual, praying along with us, as well as a deacon and perhaps I should have spoken to one of them about it afterwards but I never did. They probably would have told me to dismiss it and not think too much about it and not to discuss it. The priest was my parish priest and yet I still felt uncomfortable mentioning it to anyone, even him.

As I wrote in the Introduction, I have been greatly affected by my experiences and have kept them to myself, until now. I've been careful to safeguard my experiences. They are personal and sharing them is difficult for me. I've spent a lifetime trying to figure out why it happened to me. But I will never know that answer this side of Heaven. As I've written, which is important to stress, I have no messages to share, no warnings, no requests, and of course, no contradictions to Church teaching (to my knowledge). Nothing I will write will contradict what the Church has taught for centuries about Jesus. I do have some insights which I gleaned from the experience and from reflecting on it for years. Everything I will write, to the best of my knowledge will conform to the teachings of the Church.

When I first had a mystical experience, I did not know what the word mysticism meant. It was not a word I was familiar with. It was certainly not a word I ever heard mentioned in Church or in religion class. (I went to public school, so there was no chance of hearing that word mentioned in school.) After having what I believed was a mystical experience, I started reading about mysticism, learning the different ways it was described by theologians, mystical writers and saints. There is a lot written on mysticism, but it's not an easy word to define. Many mystical writers have stated that it's difficult to capture the essence of what mysticism is.

As William Johnston, S.J., wrote in his book on mysticism: *The Inner Eye of Love-Mysticism and Religion: It is far from easy to define the word mysticism. Writing at the end of the last century, William Ralph Inge cited no less than twenty-six different definitions of this word; and were he writing today he could cite fifty or a hundred* (p. 15).

Fr. Johnston states: *Mysticism is wisdom or knowledge that is found through love, it is loving knowledge (P.20).* He states that it is the central point of his book.

The word mystic comes from the Greek noun "mystes," which was originally connected with mystery religions and secret cults from the Greco-Roman world. Mystic comes from a Greek root and it means "mystery." The word "mysterion," (Greek *New Testament*), is related to the terms mysticism, mystic and mystery. The term mystery suggests that which is hidden and secret.

A traditional definition of mysticism is: *Experiential knowledge of God* (Hans Urs Von Balthasar). Also a very accurate definition of mysticism is: *The direct experience of God's presence.*

St. John of the Cross, Doctor of the Church (1542-1591), an extraordinary Spanish Carmelite mystical poet and writer wrote: *The sweet and living knowledge is mystical theology, that secret knowledge of God which spiritual persons call contemplation. This knowledge is very delightful because it is knowledge through love (Spiritual Canticle, 27,5).*

According to mystical writers and saints, love is the key that opens the secret door to glimpsing aspects of God's nature and essence, as limited as that will always be. And of course, prayer (in all its forms) reflection on Scripture, Christian meditation and contemplation. *Be Still and Know That I Am God* (see *Psalm 46:11*).

St. Thomas Aquinas defined mysticism (or contemplation) as: *A simple gaze on God and divine things proceeding from love......*

There are many excellent quotes on mysticism from Karl Rahner, S.J., the German Jesuit theologian, who lived in the 20th century, that were noted in the informative book: *What Are They Saying About Mysticism?* by Harvey Egan, S.J.

Karl Rahner, S.J., defined mysticism as: *Infused contemplation, in which God gratuitously makes himself known to the individual.* (*Theological Dictionary, Contemplation*)

He also wrote: *All that they experienced of closeness to God, of higher impulses, of visions, inspirations, of the consciousness of being under the special and personal guidance of the Holy Spirit, of ecstasies, etc., all this is comprised in our understanding of the word mysticism...* (*Theological Investigations 3*)

According to Karl Rahner, all mystical experience is rooted in grace and our relationship with God and the world of grace. He believed that God's self-communication is dynamic, transforming and active in this world. A key point that Rahner's theology of grace makes is that we can transcend this world and come into contact with the Absolute. I would say that for those of us who believe in God's continual outpouring of grace and mercy, which transforms and renews creation, the world is a place of infinite possibilities. Scripture would confirm that: *With God all things are possible* (see *Luke: 1:37*).

For Christian mystics, love of God is what propels them and opens them up to an intimate relationship with God, which bears "fruit," sometimes in an extraordinary way. The book, *The Cloud of Unknowing*, mentions "the blind stirring of love." St. John of the Cross speaks of "the living flame of love."

Evelyn Underhill (1875-1941) was an English poet, novelist, retreat leader and a prolific writer on mysticism. She was an expert in the field of mysticism. She was born in England and educated at Kings College for Women in London. She was raised as an Anglican but was drawn later in life to Roman Catholicism and the Catholic Mass, though she never converted. (She thought it would upset her husband.) Her first major work titled, *Mysticism,* was published in 1911 to much acclaim. It received great reviews. After the publication of the book, she befriended Baron Friedrich von Hugel who was an important Catholic scholar and writer, living in England. Another book she wrote on mysticism was published in 1915 titled, *Practical Mysticism.* The title of the first chapter begins with the question:"What is Mysticism?" This is her definition:

> *Mysticism is the art of union with Reality. The mystic is a person who has attained that union in greater or less degree; or who aims at and believes in such attainment.*

She goes on to write that the next relevant question would be, *What is Reality?* She says it's a question that will cause *infinite stress,* and it's a question only a mystic can answer and only other mystics would hope to understand.

God is an unfathomable mystery, as Karl Rahner and other theologians have said. God is what is most real. Mystics claim that they glimpse and pierce aspects of the mystery of God in a sudden revelation. Visionary mysticism or extraordinary mystical phenomena as I've experienced it, is the focus of this book. In trying to understand mysticism, one must consider the outstanding work of William James. I found his work very helpful to me on my spiritual journey.

William James was born in 1842 in New York City. His brother Henry James became a well known novelist. His sister Alice was a sensitive diarist, who suffered with psychological issues all her life. William was born into an intellectual family and he excelled and became a prominent American philosopher and a respected psychologist from Harvard University. His writings were widely read. His interest in religion came from his Swedenborgian father, who was a theologian. William delivered the famous "Gifford Lectures" at the University of Edinburgh. Those lectures make-up his classic book on the psychology of religion: *The Varieties of Religious Experience.* James begins the chapter titled, "Mysticism," by stating that though he was not prone to religious experiences he would be open-minded in his study of the subject. His case studies and those of Professor Starbuck, shed light on mystical states and religious experiences and dispel much darkness. He makes the point that religious experiences have, "a deep impression on those who have them." Authentic religious experiences are never without effects, and as

James notes in his work, experiences can be judged by the "fruit" or good they bear over time. As stated in Scripture: *So by their fruits you will know them (Mt. 7:20).*

James asserts that mystical experiences exist and they are real and valid experiences. His four marks of mysticism: "ineffability, noetic quality, transiency and passivity" are a classic treatment of mystical states. The first is "ineffability." This means that: *mystical states are more like states of feeling, than like states of intellect. No one can make clear to another who has never had a certain feeling, in what the quality or worth of it consists.* The second mark of mysticism is the "noetic quality." Mystical states are states of knowledge. *They are illuminations, revelations, full of significance and importance and as a rule they carry with them a curious sense of authority aftertime.* The third mark of mysticism is "transiency." *Mystical states cannot be sustained for long.* (That is why they are so difficult to discern.) The last characteristic he describes is that of "passivity." *....The mystic feels as if his own will were in abeyance and indeed sometimes as if he were grasped and held by a superior power* (*p.*300).

When I describe my own experience, these marks of mysticism will be helpful. James made a great contribution to the understanding of mysticism.

I have studied mysticism formally and informally. My experiences would lead me to try to search (on my own) for an explanation. I was trying to make sense of it all. In my adult years, I decided to get a Master's degree in Religion and Religious Education from Fordham University. That would be the first time in my formal education that I would take religion courses as part of a degree program. As part of the requirement for graduation from Fordham, I had to write an in-depth religion paper and I chose to research mysticism as part of that endeavor. I would search for answers to my many questions in the library at Fordham. Yet the questions I kept asking myself were: How could this be possible? Did I receive a sufficient amount of grace for the extraordinary experiences, at Baptism and Confirmation? All baptized Christians, (in a broad sense), become mystics when they are incorporated into the life of the Trinity at Baptism. Christians become part of the Communion of Saints, united to Christ and to all the baptized, all those on Earth and those living in Heaven. It's not only a comforting belief but it's also empowering.

Through Baptism and Confirmation, Christians are "claimed for Christ," "sealed in Christ" and marked with an indelible spiritual character. In the Sacrament of Confirmation, Christians are sealed with the Holy Spirit and strengthened and confirmed in baptismal graces. We "encounter" Christ in the Sacraments. Even with the knowledge of the supernatural, sacramental graces that come from the Sacraments of Baptism and Confirmation, I still kept searching for answers. Informally I have read many books and articles on the subject in my search for knowledge, clarity and truth.

The subjective, religious experience that I had, the mysterious, unusual experience of Jesus which I will describe in the coming chapters, will ultimately stand on its own. I hope you will come to see its authenticity by way of my explanation. Though words could never completely suffice and are inadequate, words and the memory of that mysterious, grace-filled event are all I have. I will use my intellect and the "light of human reason," to try to explain what happened to me. But human words can never capture its depth or mystery.

Many psychologists as well as theologians value religious experience as authentic human experience. The language, symbolism and structure may vary from person to person and from culture to culture. Many cannot find suitable words to describe their experience, yet something beyond their human ability has been experienced and they know inwardly the impact it has had on their life. It is an experience of knowing, of deep feeling, gripping awareness, awesomeness, intuitiveness and an infusion of supernatural grace. An authentic experience can also be very enlightening and increase knowledge of hidden divine truths. All authentic mystical experiences have depth and multi-faceted meaning. I recognize that mysticism and mystical experiences can happen to believers of all religions and cultures. Yet as a fully initiated Catholic Christian I had a Christian mystical experience and so this book will describe a Christian experience. My sudden, awe-filled religious experience

of the risen, exalted Christ was unexpected and unusual but it was within the framework of my beliefs. I
was oriented towards Christ through prayer and as a
fully initiated member of the Roman Catholic Church.
I prayed to the Holy Trinity. I attended Mass and wor-
shipped God. I sang hymns of adoration, sat in the presence of the Blessed Sacrament, received Eucharist at
Mass, read the Bible and prayed to Jesus. I was united
to Christ through baptism and my life of prayer and so
an experience of Christ, (if I would have any experience
at all) would make sense, given my upbringing and my
religion. (Only in hindsight and after much reflection
can I say that.)

However, it is the details of the experience, which
make it unique and it is the details which I could not
have imagined or dreamed of. It was beyond my imagination and my thought processes. That's where the supernatural element of the experience comes in. It was
my experience and I have to "own" it, because it's a part
of who I am. I was not searching for mysticism. I did
nothing extraordinary to open myself to it, but I was fully equipped, which enabled me to be open to the movement of the Spirit. I was receptive because that was part
of my nature. My heart was also open to God. I responded to the love and subtle "call" I felt from a young age.
God initiates and the Spirit of God awakens and draws
us near and a response is then necessary, for the call to
bear "fruit." As it states in Scripture: *We love because God*

first loved us (1 John 4:19)). So for me, it was there from the beginning, from when I first learned to pray. I felt connected to God through prayer. Perhaps that was what enabled me to be a vehicle for this special grace. It's the only thing I can think of that would have opened or prepared me to have this type of experience. My love for God was a part of me and my religious reality from when I was young. It was a special gift, that I was aware of, but didn't think much about. It was just me. What I did do over the years was to recognize it, accept it, respond and nurture it, while living out my life in an ordinary way. But it was still all so mysterious and unexplainable. It is part of the mystery and will always remain so.

As I mentioned earlier, I didn't seek out a spiritual director to help me discern my experiences. To put it simply, a spiritual director never crossed my path. I have had friends, deeply religious, spiritual friends throughout my life, but never anyone I felt I could confide my experiences to or share my story with. It was just too personal and too unusual and I felt uncomfortable, as I do now in writing this. I just held it in my heart, reflected upon it, studied mysticism, read and prayed with Scripture, looking for confirmation and that's what I've been doing until now. Now I'm taking a bold step.

The focus of this book as I've said, is a mystical experience based on vision that I had of the risen Christ. I will describe the vision which I believe was authentic. It would be considered mysticism in the strict sense or extraordinary mystical phenomena, or some would call it charismatic mystical phenomena, which comes from a supernatural cause, from the self-communication and revelation of God. My assumption is that the vision was authentic. It will be up to the reader of this book to decide if they agree. I believe that the vision, was a divine revelation of the Second Person of the Trinity, of Jesus Christ, Son of God and God. The knowledge I gained from the details of the vision, will hopefully convince skeptics that the origin of the vision was from God and not from any other source. There is no reason for me to think otherwise. Extraordinary mystical experiences are classified as charisms (gratiae gratis datae) and would include: visions (perceptions of God or a saint, holy person, or the Blessed Mother) voices, locutions (interior illuminations through words or statements) reading of hearts (the knowledge of the secret thoughts of others), flames of love (burning sensations in the body), exchange of hearts or mystical marriage (the mystic receives the symbolic heart of Christ or a symbolic mystical marriage to Christ), bi-location (the mystic is seen at two different places at the same time), the stigmata (the sudden appearance of the bleeding wounds of Christ on the body of a mystic), sweet odors (coming from the living or dead body of a holy person), mystical illuminations (light emanating from a mystic, which can happen during contemplation or ecstasy) and knowledge of divine truths. In the lives of some saints, there is also the phenomena known as bodily incorruptibility or the absence of rigor mortis after their death, their bodies or parts of their bodies do not become corrupted or decayed. This is considered proof of their holiness. There are other phenomena as well that are categorized as extraordinary phenomena but the ones I have named are the most well known of the extraordinary mystical occurrences.

Extraordinary mystical experiences that are authentic and come from God are for the good and benefit of the Church and the faithful. These experiences may help, inspire and motivate the mystic who has them, but from my own personal experience, I can say they are a two-edged sword and that all extraordinary mystical experiences come with "strings attached." The mystical path is a difficult one, that has been my experience. From the reading I've done on the lives of mystics, whether they were ordinary Christians, believers or canonized saints, this seems to be the case, most of the time. Having written that, I must note that the person who has a mystical experience (as was the case of St. Paul), experiences a conversion, a new way of being and they become steadfast and certain in their belief in God and zeal for the Lord.

I will end this chapter with a quote from Karl Rahner, S.J.

> *But in any case, it is true that mysticism exists and it is not as remote from us, as we are at first tempted to assume (Theological Investigations 18).*

*I saw that the glory of the Lord was in that place.
(Ezekiel 3:23)*

*I will be for her an encircling wall of fire, says the
Lord, and I will be the glory in her midst. (Zechariah 2:9)*

*The cloud covered the meeting tent and the glory of
the Lord filled the Dwelling. Moses could not enter the
meeting tent, because the cloud settled down upon it and
the glory of the Lord filled the Dwelling. (Ex.40:34-35)*

*I Daniel, alone saw the apparition....I heard him
speak and at the sound of his voice I fell unconscious to the
ground....He said then, 'Daniel, do not be afraid'.....And
as he spoke to me I felt strong again and said, 'Let my Lord
speak, You have given me strength.' (Daniel 10:7, 9, 12, 19)*

*We had been eyewitnesses of his glory.............
(2 Peter 1:16-18)*

*O God, you are my God, for you I long; for you
my soul is thirsting. My body pines for you, like a dry,
weary land without water. So I gaze on you in the sanctuary to see your strength and your glory. (Ps. 63)*

*God's temple in Heaven was opened and the Ark of
the Covenant could be seen in the Temple. (Rev. 11:19a)*

*The Bridegroom is here, go out and welcome him.
(Mt. 25:6)*

CHAPTER 4

THE VISION-THEOPHANY

Many mystical theologians and saints (such as St. Augustine) believed and stressed in their writings, that a vision of Christ, in the earthly life was possible. St. Augustine wrote: *I have sought my God in order not only to believe, but also, if possible to see something of him* (*Homily on Psalm 41*). He stressed that any vision of the, *presence of the face of God,* would be fleeting. *With the fine point of the mind we are able to gaze upon something unchangeable, although hastily and in part.*

St. Paul had a mystical vision of Christ (though he was undeserving), which completely changed his life. As he wrote, Christ appeared to him though he was, *one born abnormally, he appeared to me (1 Cor. 15:8).*

St. Teresa of Avila, St. Catherine of Siena and St. Faustina had remarkable encounters and visions of the risen Christ, as noted in a previous chapter. Their writings are fascinating and worth reading.

St. Margaret Mary Alacoque, (1647-1690), the "beloved disciple of the Sacred Heart," experienced visions of Christ, when she was a novice, in a French convent. During the third apparition, Christ showed her his human heart. She had visions that spanned a year and a half. Christ asked her to spread devotion to his Sacred Heart and gave her instructions to promote a feast day. Devotion to the Sacred Heart of Jesus was recognized by the Church, seventy-five years after her death.

The experiences of the biblical *New Testament* saints were remarkable. They saw the resurrected body of Christ, in his glorified, supernatural state, as he appeared after the Resurrection. They had many powerful, personal encounters with Christ. They spoke with him, walked with him, ate with him, "embraced his feet," and held onto him.

> *Jesus met them on their way and greeted them. They approached, embraced his feet, and did him homage (Matthew 28:9).*

According to *The Gospel of John,* St. Mary Magdalene was the first disciple to see the Risen Christ. At the entrance of the empty tomb, on the first Easter morning, St. Mary Magdalene recognized Jesus when he called her name.

Jesus said to her, 'Woman, why are you weeping? Whom are you looking for?' She thought it was the gardener and said to him, 'Sir, if you carried him away, tell me where you laid him and I will take him. Jesus said to her, 'Mary!' She turned and said to him in Hebrew, 'Rabbouni,' which means Teacher. Jesus said to her, 'Stop holding on to me, for I have not yet ascended to the Father' (John 20: 15-17).

Mary of Magdala went and announced to the disciples, 'I have seen the Lord,' and then reported what he told her (John 20: 18).

Mary Magdalene's encounter with the risen Christ is recorded in all four gospels and her personal testimony was extremely important to the early Church. What is even more incredible about St. Mary Magdalene is that in biblical times, a woman's testimony was not accepted unless verified by the testimony of men. Yet the early disciples and apostles believed in Mary Magdalene and would soon come to see proof of the Resurrection of Christ for themselves. The apostles and disciples saw the risen Christ, at different times, after the Resurrection, for forty days until He ascended into Heaven. Before seeing the risen Christ for himself, the apostle Thomas was uncertain and confused, by the stories being told of the resurrected Christ. He told the apostles:

Unless I see the mark of the nails in his hands and put my finger into the nail marks and put my hand into his side, I will not believe. (John 20:25b)

A week later, Jesus appeared suddenly to the apostles while Thomas was present and according to Scripture, Jesus spoke these words:

Thomas, put your finger here and see my hands, and bring your hand and put it into my side and do not be unbelieving, but believe. Doubting Thomas became a believer, and he replied, 'My Lord and my God!' (John 20: 27-28).

St. Thomas touched his hand and side, giving Thomas the confirmation he was seeking, that Jesus had truly risen.

In St. Luke's account of a post-Resurrection appearance Jesus stuns his apostles and disciples by showing them his glorified body and insisting he is not a ghost or spirit but he has "flesh and bones" that they can touch. Amazingly, he asks for something to eat.

While they were still speaking about this, he stood in their midst and said to them, 'Peace be with you.' But they were startled and terrified and thought that they were seeing a ghost. The he said to them, 'Why are you troubled? Why do questions arise in your hearts?

Look at my hands and my feet, that it is I myself. Touch me and see, because a ghost does not have flesh and bones as you can see I have.' As he said this he showed them his hands and his feet. While they were still incredulous with joy and were amazed, he asked them, 'Have you anything to eat?' They gave him a piece of baked fish; he took it and ate it in front of them (Luke 24:36-42).

The apostles and disciples of Jesus were the primary witnesses to the Resurrection. St. Mary Magdalene, Mary the mother of Jesus, St. Peter, St. Thomas, St. John and all the other apostles and disciples who saw the risen Christ, in his glorified body, are biblical figures and their stories are told in the Bible.

Extraordinary, highly symbolic, prophetic visions of Jesus, after he ascended to Heaven were experienced and written about by John in *The Book of Revelation*, the last book of the Bible. Scholars believe it was written between A.D. 95-96. According to Tradition, St. John the Evangelist, (the apostle who wrote St. John's gospel) was also the author of *The Book of Revelation*. Though that is disputed by most biblical scholars, the writer begins *The Book of Revelation* by noting he is "servant John." His writing is apocalyptic, highly symbolic and mystical. He described in Chapter One of being on the island of Patmos, in exile, when he received visions of Jesus. John described his first vision, occurring on a Sunday, while he was "in the Spirit."

> *I, John, your brother, who share with you the distress, the kingdom and the endurance we have in Jesus, found myself on the island called Patmos because I proclaimed God's word and gave testimony to Jesus. I was caught up 'in the Spirit' on the Lord's day and heard behind me a voice as loud as a trumpet, which said, 'Write on a scroll what you see....Then I turned to see whose voice it was that spoke to me and when I turned I saw seven gold lampstands and in the midst of the lampstands one like a son of man, wearing an ankle-length robe, with a gold sash around his chest. The hair of his head was as white as white wool or as snow and his eyes were like a fiery flame. His feet were like polished brass refined in a furnace and his voice was like the sound of rushing water....(Rv. 1:9-15).*

Other visions of Jesus followed. To fully appreciate the symbolic and prophetic nature of the visions, you would have to read through the entire *Book of Revelation,* (along with a good commentary), which would be thought-provoking and interesting.

Again caught up "in the Spirit," John has a vision:

> *At once I was caught up in spirit. A throne was there in Heaven and on the throne sat one whose appearance sparkled like jasper and carnelian. Around the throne was a halo as brilliant as an emerald. (Rv. 4:2-3)*

He also saw a vision of the Lamb of God.....

Then I saw standing in the midst of the throne and the four living creatures and the elders, a Lamb that seemed to have been slain. He had seven horns and seven eyes; these are the seven spirits of God sent out into the whole world. He came and received the scroll from the right hand of the one who sat on the throne (Rv. 5:6-7).

Visionary saints, as I've noted, have had mystical visions, in other time periods and they've described their experiences, but they're canonized saints, very holy men and women of God. They all seem far removed from the modern world that I know and live in. But apparently, ordinary baptized Christians through the grace, mercy and generosity of God can experience visions or other supernatural, religious experiences. It can happen, even in the modern world, even in an urban setting, I know it's possible, because it happened to me.

The background of the story, is fairly ordinary, or I should say at the time of the experience I'm going to describe my life was fairly ordinary. At the time of the religious experience that is the focus of this book, I was a young mother living in Brooklyn, raising my family with my husband, in the Marine Park section of Brooklyn. We were married in Good Shepherd Church on Batchelder Street in Brooklyn. When we were first married we lived in an apartment and then moved a couple of times, before we settled, in a Dutch Colonial in Marine Park, a middle- class neighborhood in Brooklyn, where we lived for almost twenty years. It was only a few blocks from where my husband and I met on East 34th Street. I lived out my childhood on East 52nd Street and then my family moved to East 34th Street when I was a teenager. It was a significant move since I would meet my husband on that block. (I continued to attend Mass at St. Columba Parish, even after I moved, as I felt comfortable in that parish.) Growing up and in early adulthood I was surrounded by middle-class, working people who strived for a better life. They wanted the same things that my parents wanted for me and my brother: solid opportunities, good schools, welcoming places of worship, nice friends, good contacts, safe streets for their children to play on. I wanted my children, growing up, to have the same experiences I had in Brooklyn, (or as similar as possible) as I found it enriching and culturally stimulating throughout my life.

I've written in earlier chapters about the "call" I felt even as a child and the "spiritual, religious attraction" that was always a part of my life. But that isn't that unusual. Millions of people are drawn towards the spiritual-religious, sacred ritual, prayer, and worship experiences. I accepted this attraction towards God and spiritual things that I always felt and I nurtured it and allowed it to grow, but that's not that unusual either. I always felt connected to God and I opened my heart to God but that's not rare either.

But what would happen one evening when I was praying in a neighborhood Church, with a Catholic

Charismatic Prayer Group would be unusual. Though I had prayed for a long time with that same group, in that same Church, under the same exact circumstances, one night would be different from the rest. Put simply, I had a subjective, mystical, religious experience, in the strict sense of the word mystical. To write, "I think I had an experience" or "I'm not sure of what I saw," would be ridiculous. I've thought about that a lot. Could I possibly write, "I'm not 100% sure of what I saw?" or "I'm not sure if it was authentic." Even though I do not understand how it could have happened to me or why, one thing I know for certain, I saw a vision of the exalted, risen, Christ. There can be no doubt in my mind about that. If you see a vision of the exalted, resurrected Christ, you can't mistake Him for anyone or anything else. It would be ludicrous to say, it was anything or anyone else. It wasn't a saint or anyone else. How can I be so sure of that? As the story unfolds I think you'll understand why. There was a divine, transcendent, holy, illuminating, powerful, noble, awe-inspiring presence to the vision that fixated and captivated my attention and focused my senses in a way, I've never experienced before. I could not move. My senses were in overload. It's hard to put into words but I was frozen, riveted, in shock. I didn't try to speak but I know I would not have been able to. I have never been so absorbed in my life. Total absorption is the only way I can describe it. I wasn't thinking of anything either. My thought process was frozen too. I am a keen observer, I like to use my intelligence and rational thought to size up situations, to observe carefully and notice what is going on around me. Well, my eyes were transfixed but I wasn't thinking what someone might think in that situation. If I could of thought logically, I would have been saying to myself: "What's going on?" "How can this be?" "What are my eyes seeing?" I was too absorb in the vision, my eyes too focused and that seemed to be using all my energy and fixating my intellect and thoughts. My body, mind and soul were totally absorbed in the vision. It was a physical perception as well as a spiritual perception. I experienced a profound, mystical, very mysterious encounter with the risen Christ, for which I was unprepared and unworthy. But that was far from my mind because I couldn't think, no less realize at the time, I was unworthy or an unlikely person for this type of experience. It's a difficult experience to put into words but I'm trying. As I mentioned in a previous chapter, one of William James' marks of mysticism is transciency. According to James, mystical experiences do not last long. That was the case for me. I do not know how long the vision lasted but it wasn't a very long time, perhaps four or five minutes. Though, it was long enough for me to grasp certain details about what I was seeing, to form memories and impressions that I would turn over and over in my mind, for many years. Many years later when I read this psalm verse, I thought to myself, this would apply to how I felt:

God is in the midst of her; she shall not be moved (Ps. 46:6).

The word "epiphany" is an unusual word, which means: a "showing, appearance, manifestation or a revelation." It comes from an ancient Greek word, "epiphanein," which was used to describe the appearance of a god or a theophany. Catholics celebrate Christ's epiphany to the world on the Feast of the Epiphany, which is an ancient feast. It is traditionally celebrated twelve days after Christmas. (In the United States the feast is celebrated on the Sunday between January 2nd and January 8th.) It celebrates Christ's light, showing and manifestation to the whole world. The gospel story of the Three Kings (also known as the Wise Men-astrologers/dream interpreters) and their long journey to bestow gifts on the newborn King of the Jews-the baby Jesus in Bethlehem, is closely related to the Epiphany feast.

Amazingly, miraculously on the day of my visitation, the day I would experience an epiphany of the Lord Jesus, I was fully awake, fully alive and alert. I was in prayer, surrounded by people of faith who were praying, in a sacred, holy place, consecrated to God, in the midst of Christian laypeople and ordained clergy. I was sitting in the presence of the Blessed Sacrament. And that was the space that Jesus chose to appear to me. The Holy One of God appeared in all his radiant beauty, as miraculous as that was.

We would gather on Friday evenings to pray in Church. I was standing in a pew praising God with a small group of worshippers. I was fully awake as it was early evening about 8:30 PM. The members of the prayer group would be sitting or standing throughout the Church, either alone or in small groups of two or three. I was alone that evening. It was a small group but very focused on prayer, praise and worship of God. Often times, our parish priest would join us and a deacon, as well as a guitarist to lead us in singing. There would be twenty to twenty-five people on a usual Friday night, invoking the power of the Holy Spirit. We would sing, praise God, listen to Scripture readings that would come from the participants, as the Spirit moved them. Towards the end, people would offer intercessory prayers for friends, family members or others. At the end of the service, people would witness how God had worked in their lives and give God glory for the prayers that had been answered.

That night was no different from any of the other Friday night the prayer group met. For me, it was the same routine on the Friday nights that I attended the prayer group. I went when I could, not every week, but most. I had rushed to Church after feeding my family dinner, cleaning up the kitchen and making sure my husband had instructions on caring for my sons. The Church was ten minutes from my house but I was usually rushing to get there, given all my responsibilities at home. (Just to make this perfectly clear, that evening or any other, I didn't drink anything alcoholic, I rarely drank. I didn't drink a lot of coffee, as I know caffeine can be a stimulant. I was not on any medication, or drugs of any kind. There was nothing in my body that physically could have affected me. I wanted to state that, as those are questions that would come to my mind, if I was reading this book.)

Catholic churches (as well as churches of other Christian denominations) are sacred spaces, each one is considered a "house of God." In a Catholic Church, the Real Presence of Jesus is present in the Blessed Sacrament, (the consecrated Host or Hosts) which are kept in the tabernacle in every Catholic Church. Consecrated hosts are kept there in reserve, for adoration of Christ but also so they can be brought to the sick and dying, as needed. The tabernacle also provides a focal point in the Church for prayer and worship. A lamp or lit candle is placed near the tabernacle, to indicate the sacredness of the tabernacle and the presence of the Blessed Sacrament there. Catholics believe the words spoken by Jesus to be true:

Where two or three are gathered together in my name, there am I in the midst of them (Matthew 18:20).

Like so many other people, who are religious or drawn to spirituality or holy mystery, being in Church has always been a comfort to me. It fills me with peace and security. The sacredness of the environment calms me and helps me to focus in prayer. I have always been moved by religious images. When I walk into a Church, whether it is empty or it is filled with people, an immediate feeling of being in a place of comfort, comes over me. The sacredness is something I was always able to feel and connect with. The psalmist sung it well:

> *O Lord, I love the house where you dwell, the place where your glory abides (Ps. 26:8).*

When I arrived at Church that particular evening, there was nothing out of the ordinary. We gathered in the vestibule until people arrived and then we moved into the Church. We prayed that the Holy Spirit would guide us and inspire us. We lifted our hands in praise and adoration of God. And then as I explained we would listen to Scripture, sing hymns and pray as the Spirit moved us. It was no different than the way thousands of prayer groups, throughout the world, pray communally and informally during praise and worship services. Sometimes they are led by a priest or deacon and other times by laypeople. Sometimes, as was the case that night, a priest and deacon were present as participants in the prayer group.

We were in the middle of the praise and worship service, adoring and praising God and asking for the inspiration of the Holy Spirit, when all of a sudden, without any "warning," Christ "came through" the statue of the risen Christ which was behind the altar. Just as the apostles claimed, after His Resurrection, that He would suddenly appear in a room, even when doors were locked, that is what happened in the vision. Suddenly, in an instant, He was present. The Sacred One was fully present. No angels singing, no bright lights, no fanfare, He was just fully present. It was as if He effortlessly, very gently and unassumingly "pierced through" or "gently passed" from one dimension to another and came into the earthly world, in the Church where we were praying. At that moment in time, Christ entered our world, for a few minutes, for reasons unknown to me and revealed Himself as the Divine One, in full glory, might, and power. But it was an unassuming power. I use the word "power" because of what He was able to do, so effortlessly, just appear, out of nowhere. In this particular Church (the Church of St. Columba) there is a life-sized figure of the risen Christ, carved in light wood, which is very imposing and beautiful. Christ's arms are raised, reaching outward. It is a statue that I loved and admired always. It is a hopeful, comforting statue, showing Christ risen, in glory. The statue is not on the floor. It is attached to the wall behind the altar and placed a few feet from the floor so that it can be seen throughout the Church. In an instant, the apparition of Christ was in front of the statue, in mid-air. He was in the space between the altar and the wall, in the sanctuary. Interestingly, as noted in the *Catechism*, "In certain Eastern liturgies, the altar is also the symbol of the tomb (Christ truly died and is risen) (see *CCC 1182*).

I wasn't afraid because my emotions were frozen, as I explained earlier, I couldn't think or feel emotion at the time on a conscious level. Interestingly, there was a "fluttering of His arms" very gentle movement, hard to describe in words but that continued throughout the vision.

The following insights into the vision, the details that I will describe are what I was able to recall after the experience. Again, I was taking it all in, transfixed and not thinking it through, while it was happening. What I'm writing now, is what I've reflected upon afterwards. I wasn't thinking then, "Oh, he's dressed like a King," or "This is a vision of Christ," or, "This is the true likeness of Christ." It wasn't' like that at all. No thoughts at all. None. I was totally immersed in the present moment, in those moments, in the "now" of time. It could not be any other way, my sight was fixed and though I didn't try to move, I'm sure I wouldn't have been able to. I was awestruck, filled with wonder and awe, motionless, absorbing and incorporating the vision into my being. Also, it was a vision only, no voice or locutions from the apparition. Nothing. What was very noticeable was the emotion coming from His face, that left an impression on me since it emanated from the vision. What emanated and was so striking was humility emanated from the face of Christ, which was a transcendent humility. It was not like any humble face I had ever seen. It was different, it poured forth in a gentle, unassuming way. It just was. It was a noble, divine humility.

Christ was dressed as a King, or as I would imagine a High Priest would dress. He was dressed nobly. The color he was wearing was an ivory color, a creamy white, not a stark white. The garment he wore was a long, kingly type robe or priestly vestment, similar to what a priest or bishop would wear, somewhat like a chasuble (the outmost sacramental garment of priests and bishops). It covered his whole body, arms included. The material was fine, like silk, I could tell that from the way it draped. His hair was covered completely. He wore a miter type-ceremonial headdress, similar to what a bishop would wear, without the point on top. It was the same color and I assume the same material as the vestment. It appeared that way. He was not holding anything. I couldn't see his hands, they were covered with the vestment/robe, but the only part of Him that I could see was His face. Just to clarify, all of what I am describing is beyond my imagination. Who could ever imagine, seeing a vision of Christ and then seeing him dressed like a King or a High Priest, in His glorified state. It is beyond anything I could have ever dreamed of. Even writing it now, I'm amazed at what I saw. It's so incredible to even be able to express this. I didn't realize how difficult it would be to write about a supernatural, mystical, religious experience. As incredible as it sounds, for a short period of time, in a sanctuary of a Roman Catholic Church in Brooklyn- St. Columba Roman Catholic Church in the Marine Park section of Brooklyn, miraculously the veil was lifted from my eyes and I saw Christ, as He truly is. I saw Christ in His true likeness: noble, kingly, priestly, exalted, risen from the dead, filled with beauty, truth and the goodness and humility of a humble, merciful God. A vision of a gentle, extraordinarily humble God who loves deeply, shows mercy abundantly and is generous beyond what we deserve. I saw the beauty and depth of Christ's humility. (....*Perfect in beauty, God shines forth (Ps. 50:2)*. It was an enlightening and transformative, grace-filled, transcendent experience for which I will ever be grateful for. There was nothing I have ever seen in my life that was more beautiful or tranquil in its being.

Fr. Hans Urs von Balthasar wrote this about beauty: *In the experience of extraordinary beauty, we are able to grasp a phenomenon that otherwise remains veiled. What we encounter in such an experience is as overwhelming as a miracle, something we will never get over.*

All of us, gazing with unveiled face on the glory of the Lord, are being transformed into the same image from glory to glory, as from the Lord, who is the Spirit (2 Cor. 3:18).

Yet God's kingdom is no distant dream or consolation; rather, it breaks into our time if we implore the Father and follow the call of Jesus (Rudolf Schnackenburg-Biblical scholar).

Humility is the most radical aspect of love. (Francois Varillon)

It seems to me that to be plunged into humility, is to be plunged into God. *(St. Elizabeth of the Trinity)*

Take my yoke upon you and learn from me, **for I am meek and humble of heart** *and you will find rest for yourselves. (Mt. 11:29)*

For the Lamb who is in the center of the throne will shepherd them and lead them to springs of life-giving water...... (Rev. 7:17)

Then the angel showed me the river of life-giving water, sparkling like crystal, flowing from the throne of God and of the Lamb.... (Rev. 22:1)

I saw no temple in the city, for its temple is the Lord God Almighty and the Lamb. The city had no need of sun or moon to shine on it, for the glory of God gave it light and its lamp was the Lamb. The nations will walk by its light, and to it the kings of the earth will bring their treasure. (Rev. 21:22-24)

━✝ ✝━

CHAPTER 5

JESUS- THE LAMB OF GOD
THE HUMILITY OF CHRIST

Long after the mystical experience I had, I came across the following quote by Meister Eckhart, who was a medieval German theologian and philosopher, he wrote: *The virtue called humility is deep-rooted in the Deity.* How correct he was. To understand the depth of the humility of God one has only to think about the Incarnation, how God became a human being and then freely and totally gave of Himself for the salvation and redemption of humankind. (The word "incarnation" means "the putting on or taking on of flesh.") Jesus' life was a total gift, given out of unconditional love and mercy. It's a remarkable story and much more than our human mind or intellect can understand or fathom.

*God is love and those who abide in love abide in
God and God abides in them (1 John 4:16b).*

The birth of Christ, which Christians celebrate on the
great feast of Christmas reveals the deep humility of
God. Jesus was not born in a castle (though he was a
descendant of King David), but in humble surroundings. God entered the world as an infant, who needed
the care and protection of human parents. Those par-
ents- his foster-father St. Joseph and his mother Mary-
the Blessed Mother, were entrusted with the care of the
Holy Infant Jesus. As St. Charles of Mount Argus wrote:
*The birth of our Lord Jesus Christ in the stable at Bethlehem is
a mystery, it is a miracle so great, abounding so much in humility and love, that it will be wondered at by the angels and saints
in heaven for all eternity.*

   When one reads St. Paul's *Letter to the Philippians*, it
speaks of how Christ emptied Himself:

*Rather, he emptied Himself taking on the form of a
slave, coming in human likeness; and found human in
appearance, he humbled himself becoming obedient to
death, even death on a cross (Phil. 2:7-8).*

Most human beings strive for recognition, honor,
achievement and status. Yet Jesus would willingly
empty Himself, by accepting the will of His Father.
He would ultimately suffer rejection, humiliation and

death on a Cross for the redemption of humankind, all out of love, obedience and fidelity. A God with such inner goodness and selflessness is hard for us to imagine. Total selflessness and sacrifice for the beloved is a gift and something poets try to capture in their writing. It's difficult to make sense of, in our human way of thinking and assessing. Unconditional love bears all for the beloved and we are the beloved, loved by God in a way that is more than we can understand. It is what it is. Love unbounded, love without limits. From the words of Scripture:

> *See what love the Father has given us, that we should be called children of God; and that is what we are (1 John 3:1).*

Children of God, beloved by God, redeemed by God, it's a gift of enormous value and if properly understood could give us much freedom and peace. If only we lived our lives each day, from the certainty of that knowledge and lived joyfully as a redeemed people, it would make a great difference in the quality of our lives. It would greatly enrich our lives and gives us meaning, purpose, joy and happiness. Words of wisdom from *Psalm 90:14*:

> *Fill us with your love that all our days we may sing with joy.*

The most remarkable aspect of the vision I saw, was the humility emanating from the face of Christ. Though difficult to put into words, one thing that struck me was the expression on Jesus' face. Using words are insufficient and limited but a deep, supernatural, appealing humility flowed from His face. A humble, extremely humble, yet exalted Christ. I have never seen such humility displayed in a human face, not even close. Christ, glorified and "without stain and reproach" perhaps just as He was when He walked on the Earth after the Resurrection (from the descriptions of the apostles and disciples). If you think of my experience as a revelation of God (as amazing as that would be), then the virtue of humility was one aspect or attribute of the divine nature that Jesus was communicating. It was the most important aspect of the whole experience. I have reflected and attempted to make sense of it, yet humility was so unmistakable, undeniable and real as it poured forth from the apparition of Christ that it stunned me. Humility holds an important place in this story. Jesus imbued with deep humility, a humility that was so natural and imbedded that it poured forth freely and naturally. It captured my attention, it was so evident and added much to Christ's beauty and being. Jesus, fully human and fully divine, is imbued with extraordinary humility, a deep, penetrating humility. It is part of His divine nature, even now, in eternity, in timelessness, in the God dimension or Heaven where He dwells. At least that's what I think after reflecting for many years on what I saw and what emotion stood out.

In the *Hebrew Scriptures* in *The Book of Isaiah*, "the suffering servant," is described in the Servant Songs, which are four poems. Christians believe the servant described by Isaiah is the prophetic figure fulfilled in Christ. In the third poem or oracle, the servant speaks:

> *The Lord has given me a well-trained tongue, that I might know how to speak to the weary a word that will rouse them. Morning after morning, he opens my ear that I may hear; and I have not turned back. I gave my back to those who plucked my beard, my face I did not shield from buffets and spitting. The Lord God is my help, therefore I am not disgraced; I have set my face like flint, knowing that I shall not be put to shame (Is. 50: 4-7).*

The servant, like Jesus, suffers extreme humiliation but does not give up. He patiently endures all the injustices and abuse. In the last of the four Servant Songs, Isaiah gives a description of a sinless servant, who atones for the sins of others:

> *Yet it was our infirmities that he bore, our sufferings that he endured. While we thought of him as stricken, as one smitten by God and afflicted. But he was pierced for our offences, crushed for our sins, upon him was the chastisement that makes us whole, by his stripes we were*

healed....Though he was harshly treated, he submitted and opened not his mouth, oppressed and condemned he was taken away and who would have thought any more of his destiny? (Isaiah 53:4-5, 7-8)

Christ achieves glory through his horrific crucifixion, death and ultimate Resurrection for our salvation. He trusts in God the Father to deliver Him and glorify Him and in the end Christ is victorious. Death and despair cannot hold its grip on Him. Christ is the victorious Lamb of God. God's mysterious will was accomplished through Christ and we are the benefactors of his generosity and selfless love. Jesus is the source of our salvation, who opened for us the path to eternal life.

For God so loved the world that he gave his only Son so that everyone who believes in him might not perish, but have eternal life (John 3:16).

It seems to me that only a God of pure humility, whose essence is radical love, would be willing to make such a sacrifice out of love. Whatever the cost, whatever the sacrifice, that was what He was willing to give. Total self-gift, for you and for me, as undeserving as we might think we are, apparently in God's eyes, we are worth the cost.

From experiential knowledge that I was blessed to gain through my sense of sight, I can attest that

God is humble and God gives generously. When Jesus walked on this earth, over two thousand years ago, He showed that over and over again through his compassionate actions and his preference for servant leadership. He made the ultimate sacrifice, the eternal sacrifice on the Cross and sealed a new covenant with his own blood.

According to *The Gospel of St. John the Evangelist* and his account of the Last Supper, Jesus creates and carries out a ritual action which astounds his apostles. In trying to teach the disciples about true humility and servant leadership he insists on washing the feet of his followers at the Last Supper, even the feet of the betrayer-Judas. This act of humble service was a show of great love and humility. The task of washing someone's feet was usually done by the lowliest of servants. Serving others with great humility and love and without condescension, are messages that Jesus gives through his words and actions at the Last Supper. Lovingly and humbly serving others is part of the gospel message and Jesus makes that very clear through his selfless actions.

I am among you, as one who serves (Luke 22:27).

As recorded in St. John's gospel:

So when he had washed their feet and put his garments back on and reclined at table, he said to them

'Do you realize what I have done for you. You call me teacher and master and rightly so, for indeed I am. If I therefore, the master and teacher, have washed your feet, you ought to wash one another's feet. I have given you a model to follow, so that as I have done for you, you should also do' (John 13:12-15).

After washing his disciples' feet, Jesus encourages and challenges his followers to practice humble service in obedience to the will of God. Jesus calls us to love, it is God's will that we love. He challenges us to go above and beyond, to do what is hard and unpleasant, at times, to fulfill the Law of Love- to love God with your whole heart, mind and soul and your neighbor as yourself. He told the apostles at the Last Supper:

I give you a new commandment: love one another. As I have loved you, so you also should love one another. This is how all will know that you are my disciples, if you have love for one another (John 13:34-35).

Love and humility are interwoven, interconnected and of great importance and value in the here and now and in the future fulfillment of God's reign.

At the time of Jesus, during the holiest of Jewish feasts-the Feast of Passover, lambs were slaughtered and sacrificed in the Temple, so that they could be brought home and eaten at the Passover meal. The blood of the lambs was also sprinkled by Hebrew priests on the altar of holocausts, a ritual to remind them of their deliverance from Egypt, after the final plague. During the feast the Jewish people recalled and memorialized the original Passover, which took place in the year 1250 B.C., when the Israelites prepared to leave Egypt, after the Ten Plagues had struck the Egyptians. The Exodus story was a pivotal event in which God intervened for his people and led them from slavery to the Promised Land. As recorded in *The Book of Exodus,* God had given Moses special instructions for the people to follow. Each family was to kill a lamb, eat it with unleavened bread and then place the blood of the lamb on the top and posts of their doorway. In doing so, the angel of the Lord would pass over their home, when striking down the firstborn of Egypt (which was the last plague). Each year the Passover feast would be celebrated, as a reminder of how God had acted on their behalf and freed them from captivity. The Jewish Passover celebrates freedom from slavery. Christians believe that through Jesus' death and Resurrection, we are freed from the power of sin and death. With great humility and obedience, Jesus became the "new paschal lamb," "the Lamb of God" whose saving blood and sacrificial death on the Cross redeemed humankind. Jesus' new covenant was sealed with his own blood. Jesus freely gave up his life and emptied himself out of love for the Father and for each of us and our salvation. The innocent and unblemished Lamb-Jesus the Lamb of God, though sacrificed, emerges victorious in the end. In St. John's gospel Jesus is referred to as the "Lamb of God" and the "new paschal lamb." St. Paul would speak of Jesus to the early Christian communities as "our Passover."

The title "Savior" for Jesus is mentioned over twenty-one times in the letters of St. Paul and in *The Acts of the Apostles.* The early Christian communities were convinced that Jesus was their Savior. They were willing to undergo persecution and brutal death rather than deny that truth.

At the beginning of Jesus' ministry, when he was about thirty years old, Jesus approached John the Baptist at the Jordon River and asked to be baptized. John was confused by the request. *I need to be baptized by you and yet you are coming to me? (Mt. 3:14)* Jesus responded: *Allow it now, for thus it is fitting for us to fulfill all righteousness (Mt. 3:15).* John's baptism was a baptism of repentance, challenging people to change their lives and repent in anticipation of the coming of the Messiah.

Make ready the way of the Lord, clear him a straight path.... All shall see the salvation of God (Luke 3:4,6).

Jesus, without sin, did not need a baptism of repentance but he submitted to baptism out of humility and to show that he identifies with all of us. John is considered a witness as portrayed in St. John's gospel. The words and prophecy of St. John the Baptist, would come true and be memorialized in the Catholic Mass.

He identified Jesus as the Lamb of God. John cried out as Jesus walked towards him:

> *Behold the Lamb who takes away the sins of the world (John 1:29).*

Since only God can forgive sin, the statement by John gives Jesus a divine title, as one who can remove sin. According to Scripture, the next day John once again recognizes Jesus as the Lamb of God, as he watched Jesus walk near him, he told others, "Behold, the Lamb of God." John was pointing to Jesus as the sacrificial lamb used at the Passover meal. The words of John the Baptist (he is also called John the Witness), pointing to Jesus as the Lamb of God, are proclaimed at every Mass, during the Communion Rite, by the priest who presides.

> *Lamb of God, you take away the sins of the world, have mercy on us. Lamb of God, you take away the sins of the world, have mercy on us. Lamb of God, you take away the sins of the world, grant us peace.*

Participants at Mass are invited to the "supper of the Lamb." The priest once again invokes the Lamb. Facing the people, he raises the host and says: *Behold the Lamb of God, behold him who takes away the sins of the world, blessed are those called to the supper of the Lamb.* The Congregation then replies that they feel unworthy but know in God's great mercy they can approach the table of the "Lamb." We are invited, to approach the altar and receive the Body and Blood of Jesus. Through the great mercy of God, we are called to come forward and be healed and experience communion with God, by receiving Holy Communion.

John the Baptist also recognized Jesus as the "suffering servant" of Isaiah's prophecy, who would *give his life as an offering for sin...and the will of the Lord shall be accomplished through him (Is. 53:10).* After he witnessed the extraordinary events that happen at Jesus' baptism:

> *I saw the Spirit come down like a dove, from the sky and remain upon him...(John 1:32).* John proclaims: *'Now I have seen and testified that he is the Son of God' (John 1:34).*

John uses the title, "Son of God," pointing out that Jesus as the Divine Son has an intimate relationship with God the Father. And yet as the second Person of the Holy Trinity, Jesus is Son and also God-Three Divine Persons in One God. The mysterious Holy Trinity is ever present in this mystical gospel.

The Holy Triduum (from the Latin meaning "three days") are the most sacred three days on the Church's calendar. The Triduum begins on the evening of Holy

Thursday, with the Mass of the Lord's Supper and ends with evening prayer on Easter Sunday. The Scriptural theme for the three day observance of the Triduum, is the symbol of the Lamb of God.

Through the sacrificial death of Christ and his Resurrection, Christianity was born. We gained much (or I should write, we gained all) through Christ's sacrifice and mediation:

> *Through the blood of Jesus we have confidence of entrance into the sanctuary (Heb. 10:19).*

We gained redemption and a means to salvation. Jesus the "unblemished, innocent lamb" atoned for our sins and opened the path to Heaven. In Christ, God's plan is fulfilled. We become children of God and heirs to the Kingdom.

The Book of Revelation, (also called "the Apocalypse") is the last book of the *New Testament*. It is written in highly symbolic, cryptic language and imagery. It was probably written to give encouragement and hope to late-first-century Christians, who were being persecuted. The message of the book is that regardless of how much suffering Christians have to endure, in the end God will be victorious and evil will be defeated.

> *Behold he is coming amid the clouds and every eye will see him (Rv. 1: 7).*

The hope of the early Christians (and a hope and belief which continues today) is that Jesus will return in glory, during the end times and bring forth God's reign. Evil forces will be destroyed once and for all. Interestingly, some fundamentalist Christians interpret the dramatic, mysterious imagery, the cryptic language, as well as the numbers, colors and "prophecies" in *The Book of Revelation* to try to decipher the exact day the world will end. This has led to much speculation and various interpretations (and many false and misleading dates throughout history), as well as much anxiety. But Jesus says clearly in Scripture: *But of that day or hour, no one knows, neither the angels in Heaven, nor the Son, but only the Father. Be watchful! Be alert! (Mark 13:32-33).* (We are to be prepared spiritually for the end times, be "awake" and ready, but not dwell on it.)

In *The Book of Revelation*, the title "Lamb" to describe Jesus is used 28 times. He is the victorious Lamb, who shares in the majesty of God the Father. Jesus as represented by a "lamb" is a depiction that comes from ancient times. The image of the victorious "lamb" is chiseled into altars, placed in stain glass windows, carved into sculptures and appears in paintings and banners in Catholic Churches throughout the world. The victorious "lamb" with a victory banner or flag with a cross, is a common representation of Jesus as the "Lamb of God.

According to tradition, St. John the Evangelist (the writer of the fourth gospel) wrote *The Book of Revelation*.

(However, many biblical scholars believe it was most likely written by a disciple of John). The author describes his motivation for writing down the prophetic message and revelation he's received. The message sent by an angel from Jesus is meant to be shared with others. He is writing, as one:

Who gives witness to the word of God and to the testimony of Jesus Christ by reporting what he saw" (Rev. 1:2).

John has several unusual visions while exiled on the island of Patmos, which was a Roman penal colony. In one of the visions, described in Chapter Five, John describes how he suddenly sees a Lamb *that seemed to have been slain.* Jesus is portrayed as a lamb with seven horns and seven eyes. But the slain lamb is living! The number seven is used often in the Bible and it is meant to signify perfection. The victorious Lamb of God is perfect. Seven horns are meant to signify his power. There is much symbolism in apocalyptic literature. Eyes are a symbol of knowledge and so Jesus the Lamb of God has knowledge of all things. Jesus, the Lamb of God is most worthy.

Each of the elders held a harp and gold bowls filled with incense, which are the prayers of the holy ones. They sang a new hymn: 'Worthy are you to receive the scroll and to break open its seals, for you were slain and with your blood you purchased for God those from every tribe and tongue, people and nation, you made them a kingdom and priests for our God, and they will reign on earth' (Rev. 5:9-10).

Countless angels, living creatures and elders surround the throne, and cry out,

Worthy is the Lamb that was slain to receive power and riches wisdom and strength, honor and glory and blessing......To the one who sits on the throne and to the Lamb be blessing and honor, glory and might, forever and ever ((Rev. 5:12-13).

For the Lamb who is the center of the throne will shepherd them and lead them to springs of life-giving water, and God will wipe away every tear from their eyes (Rv. 7:17).

These are words of hope given to the early believers to help them understand that God will always be victorious, regardless of how things may appear.

The Lamb described in *The Gospel of St. John* and in *The Book of Revelation* is victorious in the end. The Humble One that I saw, the One from whom humility poured forth in a noble, illuminating and exalted way is the Lamb once slain but now glorified. The Lamb of God is the Holy One of God, eternally one with God the Father and the Holy Spirit. This beautiful hymn of praise from *The Book of Revelation* is a prayer which can help us to keep our priorities straight, knowing we are a redeemed people and our God victorious.

> *Great and wonderful are your works, Lord God Almighty, just and true are your ways, O king of the nations. Who will not fear you, Lord, or glorify your name! For you alone are holy (Rev. 15:3-4).*

But you, Bethlehem-Ephrathah, too small to be among the clans of Judah, from you shall come forth for me one who is to be ruler in Israel; whose origin is from of old, from ancient times. (Micah 5:1)

May the kings of Tarshish and the islands bring tribute, the kings of Arabia and Seba offer gifts. May all kings bow before him, all nations serve him. For he rescues the poor when they cry out, the oppressed who have no one to help. He shows pity to the needy and the poor...... (Psalm 72:10-13a)

I am sending my messenger to prepare the way before me;

And suddenly there will come to the temple the Lord whom you seek, And the messenger of the covenant whom you desire, Yes, he is coming..... (Malachi 3:1-3)

Listen, that you may have life. I will renew with you the everlasting covenant... (Isaiah 55:3)

CHAPTER 6

CHRIST THE KING —CHRIST'S UNIQUE "KINGSHIP"

Every year in November, the Church celebrates the feast of Christ the King, on the last Sunday in Ordinary Time, just before the Season of Advent begins. Pope Pius XI established the feast in 1925. Officially it is called- the Feast of Our Lord Jesus Christ the King. The Pope saw many evils, in the world at that time and so he proclaimed, "Pax Christi in regno Christi!-The peace of Christ in the reign of Christ!" The world needed the peace of Christ, as dictatorships were on the rise and civil wars raged in many places. Respect for the Church and respect for Christ were being threatened by totalitarian regimes. In his encyclical, "Quas Primas," the Pope instituted the feast and reminded people that, "leaders and nations are bound to give respect to Christ" and the "faithful would gain strength and courage from the celebration of the feast, as we are reminded that Christ must reign in our hearts, minds, wills and bodies."

In ancient Israel, God was viewed as a king. There are many passages in the *Hebrew Scriptures*- in *The Book of Psalms* as well as the writings of the prophets, proclaiming God as king.

> *For great is the Lord and highly to be praised, to be feared above all gods. For the gods of the nations all do nothing, but the Lord made the Heavens. Splendor and power go before Him, power and grandeur are in his holy place....Bring gifts and enter his courts; bow down to the Lord, splendid in holiness. Tremble before God all the earth; say among the nations:* **The Lord is king**. *(Psalm 96:4-6, 8b-10)*

> **The Lord is king**, *robed with majesty, the Lord is robed, girded with might. ...Your throne stands firm from of old; You are from everlasting, Lord. (Psalm 93:1a-2)*

> *Your eyes will see a king in his splendor, they will look upon a vast land.......Indeed the Lord will be there with us, majestic......* **the Lord our King**, *he it is who will save us. (Isaiah 33:17, 22)*

The unique "kingship" of Christ is portrayed differently in the *New Testament* and points to the great humility, selflessness and wisdom of God. When Christians proclaim Christ as King, it takes on an entirely different meaning than what is thought of when we think of God as king or biblical kings from the *Hebrew Scriptures*.

The Israelite monarchy spanned nearly five hundred years, yet the greatest kings of ancient Israel were the first three: King Saul, King David and King Solomon. Yet these rulers, though considered great, had human flaws and disobeyed God and God's law, at different times in their lives. King Saul, the first king of ancient Israel was anointed by Samuel the prophet, but only after the seer warned Saul and the people that the king was to obey God's laws. Yet on two occasions, King Saul offended Samuel by failing to listen to instructions. Saul was a warrior king, who had military successes. But he suffered from superstition, pride, jealousy, mood swings and insecurity. He became obsessed with David and David's popularity. He considered David a political rival and planned to kill him. It says in Scripture that the prophet Samuel prophesied that God *regretted having made him King of Israel (1 Samuel 15:35).*

King David was anointed by the prophet Samuel as the second King of Israel.

The Lord said to Samuel: 'How long will you grieve for Saul, whom I have rejected as king of Israel? Fill your horn with oil, and be on your way. I am sending you to Jesse of Bethlehem, for I have chosen my king from among his sons' (1 Samuel 16:1).

Samuel obeyed the Lord, anointing David with oil to consecrate him as king. (As described in the *Hebrew Scriptures*, priests, prophets and kings were anointed with oil in a sacred ritual to set them apart to serve.) David ruled for forty years. He was greatly admired and loved as a military leader and administrator. He unified Israel (uniting all twelve tribes of Israel into one nation) and helped make it a formidable nation. He defeated the Philistines and conquered the surrounding land. He was a talented musician and poet. Jerusalem, the new capital, became the "city of David." He was credited with bringing the Ark of the Covenant to Jerusalem. Yet he also abused his power and turned away from God and the commandments, forgetting God who had greatly blessed him. The deadly sin of pride, as well as selfishness and lust caused David to commit adultery with Bathsheba, devise an evil plan and have Uriah, her husband killed in battle. David repented and cried: *I have sinned against the Lord (2 Samuel 12:13).* For all his faults and failures, he is still honored as the greatest King of Israel.

Christians believe that Jesus is a direct descendent of King David, according to the genealogies of *St. Matthew (1:2-16) and St. Luke (3:23-38)* and the words of St. Paul proclaiming: Jesus *was descended from David according to the flesh (Rom.1:3)*. The early Fathers of the Church taught that since people usually married within their clan, Joseph as well as Mary belonged to the House of David. Jesus is often referred to in the *New Testament* as the "Son of David." St. Matthew used the title at least seven times in his gospel, but the other gospel writers used it as well. The pleading cry of the blind beggar, Bartimaeus as recorded in St. Mark's gospel, stresses the point. He cried: *Jesus, Son of David, have pity on me! (Mark 10:47)*.

King Solomon, David's son and successor, was a wise and wealthy king as well as a great builder. He opened up trade routes and brought great wealth to ancient Israel. Two magnificent palaces and Solomon's Temple (the first Temple in Jerusalem) were built during his reign. The Temple in Jerusalem would provide a permanent home for the Ark of the Covenant (a wooden box that held the tablets of the Ten Commandments). The Temple also provided an impressive place of worship for the Israelites. Priests had many roles to play in the Temple, as the priests offered sacrifices in the Temple, and were intermediaries between the Israelites and God. Yet even the Temple priests and the High Priest could not keep King Solomon from idolatry. King Solomon suffered from human frailty and the consequences of idolatry. Power can corrupt and it "cast its spell" on King Solomon. The wise king fell into sin. He built shrines to false gods to appease his foreign wives. He also took part in idol worship, disobeying God and the First Commandment which states: *You shall not have strange gods before* me. The nation of Israel would suffer from his sins and the sins of the people, (as some would believe). The kingdom became divided after his death (the kingdom split in two, into the northern kingdom of Israel and the southern kingdom of Judah). Restoration would come, but not easily. It would be three centuries between King Solomon's reign and the restoration.

People sometimes associate secular, earthly kings, with oppression, domination, injustice, abuse of power and great wealth. Yet, throughout history there have also been kind, generous, just and benevolent kings as well. Yet Jesus was set apart, by God the Father, to be the greatest, most compassionate and humble servant/king who ever lived. Jesus redefined kingship. Jesus as God Incarnate was a "king" who was born in a simple, unpretentious stable, in poor surroundings. He was never corrupted by power, prestige, pride or wealth. Jesus was a "king" who lived simply and died a humiliating and sacrificial death on the Cross, for the salvation of the world. He brought freedom, depth, the promise of a meaningful life on earth and eternal life to humankind- to all who would listen to his radical call to love and to serve. Jesus' "kingship" cannot be compared to any other.

Jesus lived, taught and proclaimed something entirely new and different, from what the world had ever experienced in kingship. Jesus as the *wisdom and power of*

God, transformed and elevated "kingship." Jesus' "kingship" was one of love, mercy, justice, humility, compassion and service. Jesus' compassion was felt deep within him and moved him. The word "compassion" is formed from "passio" which means to suffer and "com" which means together with.

Jesus taught his disciples about servant leadership and self-emptying love in the following passage from the *New Testament:*

> *Jesus summoned them and said to them, 'You know that those who are recognized as rulers over the Gentiles lord it over them and their great ones make their authority over them felt. But it shall not be so among you. Rather, whoever wishes to be great among you will be your servant; whoever wishes to be first among you will be the slave of all. For the Son of Man did not come to be served but to serve and to give his life as a ransom for many' (Mark 10:42-45).*

In this passage, Jesus turns worldly power and dominion upside down. Jesus came to serve, not to be served and the same would be expected of his disciples. Jesus did not need great wealth, or a dominating presence to bring forth the Reign of God or to teach what's important to God. Jesus' kingship depends on love, mercy, compassion and the truth, to bring about transformation and conversion in others.

Jesus is a leader who teaches, guides, and shows the way, out of love, because of his deep love and concern for us. Jesus is firm, in that he does expect his disciples to listen and try to grasp his radical message of love and service and put his teachings into practice, so as to bring forth the Reign of God (in the here and now and in the future as well).

I gained insights into the importance of listening in prayer and the number of times it's mentioned in Scripture from Augustine Ichiro Okumura's insightful book, "Awakening To Prayer."

Jesus stresses the importance of listening, over and over again in his teachings. Attentive listening is the key to true discipleship. The word "listen" appears 425 times in the *New Testament*. He said to his disciples: *Whoever has ears ought to hear (Mt. 11:15).* In John's gospel, Jesus says:

> *My sheep hear my voice; I know them and they follow me. I give them eternal life and they shall never perish (John 10:27-28).*

The wise, mindful and attentive disciple puts Jesus' words into action. For those who do not listen, there can be dire consequences.

> *Everyone who listens to these words of mine and acts on them will be like a wise man who built his house on rock. The rains fell, the floods came, and the winds*

blew and buffeted the house. But it did not collapse; it had been set solidly on rock. (Mt. 7:24-25).

(The word "listen" is also important in the *Hebrew Scriptures* where it appears more than 1,000 times.)

In the Passion account from *The Gospel of John*, Jesus tells Pilate that his kingdom is not of this world. Pilate questions Jesus to which Jesus replies:

> *'My kingdom does not belong to this world....As it is, my kingdom is not here'....So Pilate said to him, 'Then you are a king?' Jesus answered, 'You say I am a king. For this I was born and for this I came into the world, to testify to the truth. Everyone who belongs to the truth, listens to my voice' (John 18:36-37).*

Christ is a king but he's clearly a different kind of king. He identifies with the hungry, the poor and neglected. He is a king who emanates humility, supernatural or other-worldly humility and deep compassion. Jesus said of himself: *I am meek and humble of heart (Matthew 28:29b).*

In *The Gospel of Matthew*, when the time of judgment comes and Jesus returns in glory, his followers will be judged on how well they served the poor, fed the hungry, clothe the naked, visited the imprisoned and served the less fortunate, as they were called to. Jesus' words challenged them to do more and the challenge remains for his followers today.

When the Son of Man comes in his glory, and all the angels with him, he will sit upon his glorious throne and all the nations will be assembled before him. And he will separate them one from another, as a shepherd separates the sheep from the goats. He will place the sheep on his right and the goats of his left. Then the king will say to those on his right, 'Come, you who are blessed by my Father. Inherit the kingdom prepared for you from the foundation of the world. For I was hungry and you gave me food, I was thirsty and you gave me drink, a stranger and you welcomed me, naked and you clothe me, ill and you cared for me, in prison and you visited me.' Then the righteous will answer him and say, 'Lord when did we see you hungry and feed you, or thirsty and give you drink? When did we see you a stranger and welcome you or naked and clothe you? When did we see you ill or in prison, and visit you? And the king will say to them in reply, 'Amen, I say to you, whatever you did for one of these least brothers of mine, you did for me.' Then he will say to those on his left, 'Depart from me you accursed, into the eternal fire.....For I was hungry and you gave me no food, I was thirsty and you gave me no drink, a stranger and you gave me no welcome, naked and you gave me no clothing, ill and in prison, and you did not care for me. Then they will answer and say, 'Lord when did we see you hungry or thirsty or a stranger or naked or ill or in prison and not minister to your needs?' He will answer them, 'Amen, I say to you, what you did not do for one of these least ones, you did not do for me.' And these will go off to eternal punishment, but the righteous to eternal life (Matthew 25:31-46).

This is the Christ-King I saw. A humble and compassionate king, wearing a simple ivory-colored garment (though the fabric seemed luxurious- either silk or silk-like). But there was no gold or silver ornaments or trim, no jewels or sparkle, just a simple yet beautiful and well draped robe or vestment, which was long-sleeved, covering his arms too. No jeweled crown or crown of any type but a simple miter, without the point (A pointed miter is what Catholic bishops commonly wear). No throne, no scepter and orb, just plain beauty. Oh yes, Jesus was quite beautiful. It would be hard to put into words. I know beauty when I see it. I have an appreciation for beauty. I have visited many spectacular museums in the world. Living near New York City I often go to the Metropolitan Museum of Art and other museums. I have an appreciation and admiration for great art, for artistic masterpieces. I also appreciate the beauty of nature. I can write with certainty that I was in the presence of pure, divine beauty, pure truth. Beauty that can't be adequately described in words because it was not of this world. The apparition I saw was peaceful, gentle, beautiful and non-threatening. His humble countenance did not show any condescension or superiority. No pride, no loftiness, nothing but humility and gentleness is what I saw. There is no condescension in radical love.

Who is this that comes forth like the dawn, as beautiful as the moon, as resplendent as the sun? (Song of Songs 6:10)

Christ as King would fulfill the prophecies of old. The fulfillment of *Psalm 72:10*, the prophecy of Micah (5:1), which foretold of Jesus' birth in Bethlehem and other ancient prophecies were fulfilled in the birth of the Christ. Jesus' birth in Bethlehem is significant as the birthplace of Jesus, since Bethlehem is the place David was anointed king (see *Samuel 16:1-13*).

The prophet Isaiah proclaimed:

Caravans of camels shall fill you, dromedaries from Midian and Ephah; All from Sheba shall come bearing gold and frankincense and proclaiming the praises of the Lord (Is. 60:6).

The story of the visit of the Magi is found only in Matthew's gospel.

When Jesus was born in Bethlehem of Judea, in the days of King Herod, behold, magi from the east arrived in Jerusalem saying, 'Where is the newborn king of the Jews? We saw his star at its rising and have come to do him homage' (Matthew 2:1-2).

The three Magi have been referred to as Three Kings, astrologers, Wise Men from the East, or dream interpreters with an expert knowledge of the night sky. They clearly were aware of the movement of the stars. In the ancient world, it was believed that an unusual celestial event would occur, at the time of the birth of a king. These wise men followed a brilliant star (apparently it was so bright, it was rare) until they found Jesus in a stable, with Mary and Joseph. These wise men were the first to pay homage and worship Christ as King. According to Scripture, they brought gifts of gold, (fitting for a king), frankincense and myrrh.

In St. Luke's gospel account of the birth of Jesus, the first to hear the message of the angels, were lowly, poor shepherds. God's revelation is for all to hear and be a part of, including the lowly, the outcasts and the poor. The angel of the Lord appeared to the shepherds, and proclaimed to them:

> *Do not be afraid, for behold, I proclaim to you good news of great joy that will be for all the people. For today in the city of David, a savior has been born for you who is Messiah and Lord. And this will be a sign for you: you will find an infant wrapped in swaddling clothes and lying in a manger. And suddenly there was a multitude of the heavenly host with the angel, praising God and saying, 'Glory to God in the highest and on earth peace to those on whom his favor rests' (Luke 2:10-14).*

According to Scripture, when Jesus entered Jerusalem triumphantly, (celebrated on Palm Sunday), riding on a humble and peaceful donkey, the cries of the people would be similar to the angelic voices, who announced his birth.

> *As he rode along, the people were spreading their cloaks over the road. When he approached the slope of the Mount of Olives, the whole multitude of his disciples began to praise God aloud with joy for all the mighty deeds they had seen. They proclaimed: 'Blessed is the king who comes in the name of the Lord. Peace in Heaven and glory in the highest' (Luke 19:36-38).*

In John's gospel, the crowd cries:

> *Hosanna! Blessed is he who comes in the name of the Lord, the King of Israel" (John 12:13).*

The "Davidic Messiah," the "Prince of Peace," the "Son of Man," the "King of Israel," had entered Jerusalem amid much rejoicing. Christians believe that the prophetic oracle of Zechariah would be fulfilled in this event. The prophet Zechariah, as recorded in the *Hebrew Scriptures* would proclaim in approximately 520 B.C.,

> *Rejoice heartily, O daughter Zion, shout for joy, O daughter Jerusalem! See, your king shall come to you; a just savior is he. Meek and riding on an ass (Zech. 9:9).*

Jesus was a "powerful king" in that he showed God's power, combined with mercy. Jesus could act in supernatural ways that defied the laws of nature. His miraculous signs and miracles astounded his apostles and followers and shed light on his Divine nature. The word "dynamis" in Greek means "an act of power" and that is what many of his actions showed in the *New Testament.* Throughout his ministry, his followers witnessed miracles for which there were no logical explanations. As recorded in the gospels, they witnessed extraordinary, miraculous events such as Jesus: changing water into wine, healing the sick and disabled, forgiving sins, driving out demons, calming the sea, walking on water, raising the dead to life, making predictions about his future suffering, death and resurrection and having supernatural, prophetic knowledge of other people. The Samaritan woman was humbled when he told her: *You have had five husbands and the one you have now is not your husband"* ((John 4:16), or when he told his apostles*: Did I not choose you twelve? Yet is not one of you a devil?* (referring to Judas Iscariot-the betrayer) *(John 6:70).*

Jesus' spoke continually about the kingdom of God. The kingdom of God was fulfilled in his coming and was the purpose of his mission. He would proclaim throughout Galilee:

> *This is the time of fulfillment. The kingdom of God is at hand. Repent and believe in the gospel" (Mk. 1:14-15).*

In the person of Jesus, the kingdom was realized yet its total fulfillment will come at the end of time, when Jesus returns in glory. Jesus tried to use parables to teach his followers that the kingdom of God meant living a new life with God and others and waiting expectantly for the total and complete fulfillment of the kingdom. In one parable, Jesus spoke of a merchant looking for precious pearls.

> *The kingdom of God is like a merchant searching for fine pearls. When he finds a pearl of great price, he goes and sells all he has and buys it" (Matthew 13:46).*

The kingdom has great worth, it brings great happiness and fullness of life. It's worth seeking with all one's heart. Whenever we act with justice, kindness, compassion and love we are working to bring forth the kingdom or reign of God in its totality. We each have a part to play, carefully using our words, deeds and prayer to bring it to total fulfillment at the end of the age. Whenever we serve others, with humility and Christ-like compassion the kingdom is present.

Jesus challenged and confronted religious leaders and exercised his authority and power when pushed to do so. The hypocrisy of the scribes and Pharisees drove him to insult them with harsh words and criticism:

> *Woe to you, scribes and Pharisees, you hypocrites. You are like white-washed tombs, which appear beautiful on the outside but inside are full of dead men's bones and every kind of filth. Even so, on the outside you*

appear righteous but inside you are filled with hypocrisy and evildoing (Matthew 23:27-28).

He didn't mince words! Jesus was furious with the money-changers in the temple and even overturned tables, telling the temple leaders that the temple was a "house of prayer." What infuriated Jesus? The Temple in Jerusalem was the most sacred place in Jerusalem and there he found: *those who sold oxen, sheep and doves.....He made a whip out of cords and drove them all out of the Temple area".......He overturned tables.....and He said, 'Stop making my Father's house a marketplace!' (John 2:15-16).*

The night that I saw the apparition of Jesus, his Father's "house of prayer" was just that. He appeared amidst his people who were praying, giving praise to God in joyful song, witnessing to God's power, freely expressing love, thanks and raising their hearts and minds to God. I would imagine the "Prince of Peace" was pleased with what He saw and heard during His unexpected visit. The veil was lifted and I saw Him there, in His glorified state, looking very dignified, dressed in sacred garments, yet very much at peace.

The "Messianic-Davidic King" is meek, gentle and humble and that is what my eyes saw, when the veil was lifted from my eyes and I was able to clearly see. I was given a great gift and I will never understand why. My response always has to be one of gratitude and awe at the great mercy and generosity of God.

God made him perpetual in his office, when he bestowed on him the priesthood of his people. He established him in honor and crowned him with lofty majesty. (Sirach 45:7)

Through the blood of Jesus we have confidence of entrance into the sanctuary. (Heb. 10:19)

In times past, God spoke in partial and various ways to our ancestors through the prophets; in these last days, he spoke to us through a son whom he made heir of all things and through whom he created the Universe… the very imprint of his being……… and who sustains all things by his mighty word. When he accomplished purification from sins, he took his seat at the right hand of the Majesty on high………. (Hebrews 1:1-4)

CHAPTER 7

CHRIST-THE ETERNAL HIGH PRIEST

Jesus is the one, true, holy, priest. But Jesus is no ordinary priest. Jesus Christ, the God-Man, is the eternal High Priest sent by God the Father to be our Intercessor and Mediator, as well as our Savior and Redeemer. Jesus is a mediator between God and humankind and because he was sent by the Father, as a mediator, in solidarity with human beings, (being human he could identify with us), Jesus is entitled to be called the Great High Priest. Jesus was called, anointed and appointed by God the Father to atone for our sins, a mission he willingly accepted. That is a great mystery but Christians accept it with faith. We have been given fullness of life through Christ.

In this way the love of God was revealed to us: God sent his only Son into the world, so that we might have life through him (1 John 4:9).

Fullness of life, a life full of meaning and depth comes through Jesus Christ. Jesus opened for us a path of intimacy with God the Father. Like Zechariah, (the father of John the Baptist) prophesied, filled with the Spirit, we should joyfully proclaim:

Blessed be the Lord, the God of Israel, for he has visited and brought redemption to his people (Luke 1:68).

As is written in this passage from *The Letter to the Hebrews* in the *New Testament*:

He had to become like his brothers, in every way, that he might be a merciful and faithful high priest before God to expiate the sins of the people. Because he himself was tested through what he suffered, he is able to help those who are being tested (Hebrews 2:17-18).

Jesus became like us ("in all things but sin"), he was perfected through his suffering, enabling him to fully identify with the human condition. Jesus- fully human and fully divine -was able to offer the perfect sacrifice because he was perfected through temptation, despair, rejection and suffering.

It is interesting to note that the High Priests of ancient Israel, who held the highest position in the Temple came from the Tribe of Levi and were descendants of Aaron (the brother of Moses). They were anointed in the same way that kings were. Also, they dressed in colorful, fine clothing, with ornate trim. Gold thread as well as violet, purple and scarlet yarns were used for embellishment. They wore a breastplate made of precious stones. In *The Book of Exodus*, in the *Hebrew Scriptures*, in Chapter 28 it describes how High Priests were to dress. They wore holy vestments and miters. They were given exact instructions on how their clothing and miter should be worn. For example:

> *You shall also make a plate of pure gold and engrave on it, as on a seal engraving, 'Sacred to the Lord.' This plate is to be tied over the miter with a violet ribbon in such a way that it rests on the front of the miter, over Aaron's forehead. Since Aaron bears whatever guilt the Israelites may incur in consecrating any of their sacred gifts, this plate must always be over his forehead, so that they may find favor with the Lord. The tunic of fine linen shall be brocaded. The miter shall be made of fine linen... (Exodus 28:36-39).*

The High Priests had great influence, wealth and prestige. They were responsible for Temple services and sacrifices in the Temple and their holiness and purity were extremely important to the Israelite community. It was the High Priest alone who could enter the Holy of Holies, once a year, on the Day of Atonement. It is written in *The Book of Leviticus:*

> *The most exalted of the priests upon whose head the anointing oil has been poured and who has been ordained to wear the special vestments, shall not bear his head or rend his garments....(Lev. 21:10). It* is mentioned in Chapter 10 as well that Aaron and his sons should not "bare their heads (Lev. 10:6).

Jesus is the compassionate High Priest, in union with humanity, and through His sacrifice He lifts us all and gives to us endless possibilities to be in communion with God and to reach true fulfillment as human beings.

> *For it was fitting that he, for whom and through whom all things exist, in bringing many children to glory, should make the leader to their salvation perfect through suffering. (Hebrews 2:10).*

Jesus as the compassionate High Priest identifies with the human condition, he understands suffering, rejection, hurts and pain. Though he is set apart, He is one with us, God with us.

Jesus as the Eternal High Priest offered himself for the salvation of others. He did so willingly. He took upon himself sin, despair and suffering, so that we might be set free. Jesus' sacrificial death on the Cross, set us free from the slavery of sin and death, thus achieving our salvation. Jesus not only "revealed" the Father but opened a path to the Father as well. Jesus' sacrificial death was a gift: a merciful gift, filled with unconditional love, a gift greater than we can imagine. St. Paul wrote in his letter to the Ephesians:

> *In him we have redemption by his blood, the forgiveness of transgressions, in accord with the riches of his grace that he lavished upon us. In all wisdom and insight he has made known to us the mystery of his will..... (Ephesians 1:7-9).*

Grace has been lavished upon us through Jesus Christ. And mercy has been lavished upon us as well. We only have to be grateful, receptive and open to these remarkable blessings and abundant grace.

Jesus as the Great High Priest became both priest and the sacrifice offered.

> *It was fitting that we should have a high priest: holy, innocent, undefiled, separated from sinners, higher than the heavens. He has no need, as did the high priests to offer sacrifice day after day, first for his own sins and then for those of the people; he did that once and for all when he offered himself ((Hebrews 7:26).*

Jesus was the "perfect" sacrifice and gave the ultimate sacrifice out of love. At Mass, Catholics believe they take part, mystically, in the original sacrifice of Christ. It is referred to as a "oneness in time." The Mass makes present for us, the one sacrifice that happened at Calvary. (See *Catechism of the Catholic Church* # 1367)

We have been redeemed out of love. The saints (St. Augustine and St. Therese of Lisieux mentioned this in their writings), tell us that God loves each soul as if there were no other. It's a very personal love and this is the love that Jesus showed to us through the Incarnation-taking human form and then willingly suffering for our sins. As it says in St. Luke's gospel, Jesus came: *to seek and save what was lost (Luke 19:10).* As the great Hebrew prophet Isaiah prophesied about the "Suffering Servant," Jesus would be *pierced for our offenses.* Through the Resurrection He gave us total freedom, the promise of new life and a link to the Father. It is difficult to truly understand how Christ's Incarnation and ultimate sacrifice on the Cross opened the path to the Father, to the transcendent God. Jesus was the mediator who made the connectedness to God the Father a reality.

He is always able to save those who approach God through him, since he lives forever to make intercession for them (Hebrews 7:25). He is the mediator of a new covenant: *For this reason he is mediator of a new covenant since a death has taken place for deliverance from transgressions under the first covenant, those who are called may receive the promised eternal heritance (Hebrews 9:15).*

Jesus established the New Covenant with his own blood. We learn from the *Hebrew Scriptures*, that Moses, the great prophet and lawgiver of the ancient Israelites, made a covenant with God and received the Law, on Mount Sinai, which included the Ten Commandments. The Israelite people promised to obey the Law and to worship God and remain in right relationship with God. (The Ten Commandments remain an important moral teaching for both Jews and Christians.) According to *The Book of Exodus*, they said in agreement: *All that the Lord has said, we will heed and do (Exodus 24:7b).* The covenant was sealed with the blood of young bulls. Moses poured the animals' blood on the altar and also sprinkled blood on the Israelites, according to an ancient ritual. Moses spoke these words: *This is the blood of the covenant, which the Lord has made with you in accordance with all these words of his (Ex. 24:8).*

The New Covenant that Jesus established with his own blood, became the way to fulfillment and communion with God and completed the "perfect sacrifice" of Christ. It also fulfilled the prophecy of Jeremiah:

The days are coming says the Lord, when I will make a new covenant with the house of Israel and the house of Judah...This is the covenant which I will make with the house of Israel....I will place my law within them and write it upon their hearts, I will be their God and they shall be my people (Jeremiah 31:31,33).

When Catholics partake of the Body and Blood of Christ at Mass, they share in the New Covenant. Christ fulfilled the Old Covenant through his blood and sacrificial death on the Cross. As it states in the *Catechism*: *Everything that the priesthood of the Old Covenant prefigured finds its fulfillment in Jesus Christ* (CCC #1544). As is written in *The Letter to the Hebrews,* Jesus after he was perfected:

He became the source of eternal salvation for all who obey him, declared by God, high priest according to the order of Melchizedek (Heb. 5:9-10).

Who exactly is Melchizedek? Melchizedek, was the ancient king-priest of Salem (ancient name for Jerusalem) who is a mysterious figure in the *Hebrew Scriptures.* He is mentioned in *The Book of Genesis,* as blessing Abram, after he returns from a victorious battle and bringing Abram bread and wine. This offering from Melchizedek with words of praise for God: *Blessed be Abram by God most High, the creator of Heaven and Earth, and blessed be God Most High, who delivered your foes into your hands (Genesis 14:19-20),* is believed by biblical scholars to prefigure (foreshadow) Christ's offering, which would become His Body and Blood in the Eucharist. So there is a connection, a link between the priest/king Melchizedek of the *Hebrew Scriptures* and the priest/king/Messiah of the *New Testament*. They both offer praise to God the Father, they both offer bread and wine in the holy city, though at different times in salvation history.

During the Bread of Life Discourse in *The Gospel of John,* the Evangelist wrote about Jesus teaching the crowds, that His Father gave the ancient Israelites manna in the desert, but He is: *The bread of God is that which comes down from Heaven and gives life to the world.* Jesus states emphatically: *I am the bread of life, whoever comes to me will never hunger and whoever believes in me will never thirst (John 6:33-35).*

Jesus goes on to say as written in John's gospel that: *Whoever eats my flesh and drinks my blood has eternal life and I will raise him on the last day. For my flesh is true food and my blood is true drink. Whoever eats my flesh and drinks my blood remains in me and I in him (John 6:54-56).* Those statements were difficult to understand (one of the "hard" sayings of Jesus) and it says in Scripture even his own disciples said: *This saying is hard, who can accept it? (John 6:60b).* The problem was for an Israelite there was a prohibition against drinking blood which came from the *Hebrew Scriptures* in *Leviticus 17:10-14.* Moses was told by the Lord to give instructions to Aaron and his sons regarding the offering of animals as a sacrifice. Blood was considered sacred, as a sign of life, even the blood of an animal. God gave strict instructions, which included a serious warning: *If anyone from the house of Israel or of the aliens residing among them partakes of any blood I will set myself against that one who partakes of blood and will cut him off from among his people. Since the life of a living body is in its blood, I have made you put it on the altar so that the atonement may be made for your own lives because it is the blood as the seat of life, that makes atonement (Lv:17:10-11).* Jesus would become the everlasting atonement, but it was difficult for his apostles and disciples to understand because a new age, a new covenant was being ushered in by Jesus and so their confusion is understandable. It would take them time to fully comprehend the new thing that God was doing in their midst.

When I observe people at Mass, going up to receive Holy Communion, I am always edified by their belief in the true presence. When Catholics partake of the Body and Blood of Christ at Mass, they are saying "Amen," "Yes I believe," this is the "Body, Blood, Soul and Divinity of Jesus." It's really remarkable when you think about it.

The words that are spoken at Mass, during the Eucharistic Prayer, proclaimed by the priest: *Take this, all of you, and drink from it; for this is the chalice of my blood, the blood of the new and eternal covenant, which will be poured out for you and for many for the forgiveness of sins. Do this in memory of me,* should be a reminder to all Catholics of the everlasting covenant that we are blessed to be part of. Our prayerful stance should be one of gratefulness and awe for the great gift we have been given in Christ and his eternal priesthood. And from his eternal priesthood comes, communion with God and the gift of eternal salvation.

In Chapter 8 of *The Letter to the Hebrews,* Christ is called a *minister of the sanctuary and of the true tabernacle.....(Heb. 8:2).*

> *The main point of what has been said is this: we have such a high priest, who has taken his seat at the right hand of the throne of the Majesty in heaven, a minister of the sanctuary and of the true tabernacle that the Lord, not man set up (Heb. 8:1-2).*

In the *New Collegeville Bible Commentary* on *The Letter to the Hebrews* by Daniel Harrington, S.J., he states the following regarding this passage: *The sanctuary where Christ ministers has been established by God, not by human beings. It is therefore the 'true tabernacle' in the sense that every earthly sanctuary is a copy and shadow of the heavenly sanctuary (p. 36).* This is very important as I try to find meaning and explanation for the vision I had of the Risen Christ as the Great High Priest. Jesus appeared in the sanctuary of the Church, where I was praying with a prayer group. It was if he made the transition from the heavenly sanctuary to the earthly sanctuary without effort or strain. I'm trying to use words and words will never capture it adequately, but Jesus appeared to come through another dimension (from the heavenly sanctuary?) quietly, silently, peacefully and the only movement was the fluttering of his arms beneath his sacred robe/vestment. Aside from the emotion which emanated from his face, it was a very peaceful apparition. Christ was totally in control of the situation (and dare I write, seemingly very comfortable in the surroundings). I was the observer and for whatever reason, at that moment in time, in that Church, he appeared suddenly, just like that, in a supernatural way, defying the laws of nature.

What makes me think that I saw an image of Jesus as the Great High Priest? He appeared in the sanctuary. That's very significant. He appeared in the Holy of Holies, in the most sacred place in the Church. Can it be that he fulfilled the Scripture passage from *The Letter to the Hebrews* and as "minister of the sanctuary" he appeared in the earthly sanctuary, to show that he was "Lord and High Priest" of the sanctuary of the Church? Could it be that the following Scripture verse was fulfilled : *Then God's temple in heaven was opened and the Ark of the Covenant could be seen in the Temple. There were flashes of lighting, rumblings and peals of thunder, an earthquake and a violent hailstorm (Rev. 11:19).* The actual Ark of the Covenant was lost, hidden or destroyed when Solomon's temple was destroyed in 587 B.C. Cosmic signs were seen as mentioned in Scripture, as the heavenly temple opens. Could Jesus descend into the Holy of Holies into the earthly realm and take his place where the Ark of the Covenant would be? Would He appear in silence, without fanfare or cosmic signs? A fascinating idea to reflect upon.

What other reason would I have for thinking I saw an apparition that portrayed Jesus as the Great High Priest? The other reason for concluding that is because of what Jesus was wearing. He was wearing on his head, what appeared to be a simple miter-like head covering, in an ivory-whitish color. (It was not stark white.) It did not have any ornaments, jewels, embroidery or trim. It completely covered his head. The fabric was either silk or fine silken linen. It seemed like a fine fabric. Unlike the miter that Catholic bishops wear, there was no point on the miter. The sacred vestment or robe that he was wearing was the same fabric and color as the miter-like head covering. It draped beautifully. It was elegant. It was long and covered his whole body, including his arms. That is what I remember, what has been seared into my memory. Other than his face, which was quite beautiful, he was completely covered with sacred vestments/robe and a miter-like headdress. Interestingly, in the Catholic Church, according to Canon Law, only the pope, cardinals, or bishops can wear a miter. Also, with special papal privilege some abbots and prelates are given the privilege to wear a miter, though that is not a common practice.

Jesus, the Messianic High Priest, was alone given the divine task to be the "mediator of the new covenant." Only Christ could bring this about. This is confirmed in *The Acts of the Apostles*: *There is no salvation through anyone else, nor is there any other name under heaven given to the human race by which we are to be saved (Acts 4:12).* Only Christ could have brought this to fruition. And only out of supernatural and unconditional love for each one of us, depth of love that is beyond human comprehension.

Jesus as the Great High Priest embodies divine holiness. He became the holy sanctuary of the Temple. *The Word became flesh and made his dwelling among us, and we saw his glory, the glory as of the Father's only Son, full of grace and truth" (John 1:14).* Just as the Jerusalem Temple was the place for the ancient Israelites where God's holiness and presence dwelled, Jesus became the embodiment of God's glory and God's presence among his people in his Divine Being. A humble, gentle holiness emanated from him.

I will end this chapter with the following passage from *The Letter to the Hebrews*:

> *Through him let us continually offer God a sacrifice of praise, that is, the fruit of lips that confess his name. Do not neglect to do good and to share what you have; God is pleased by sacrifices of that kind (Hebrews 13:15-16).*

Giving praise to God through prayer is pleasing to God and will keep us in right relationship with God. But there's more to it. We should strive to do good and share our blessings and resources with others in need. Those are the sacrifices that are most pleasing to God, when we act upon the words of Jesus and help the less fortunate and the most vulnerable among us.

If Christ has not been raised, your faith is in vain...
(1 Cor. 15:17)

Where, O death, is your victory? Where, O death, is your sting? (1 Cor. 15:55)

Why do you seek the living one among the dead? He is not here, he has been raised. (Luke 24:5-6)

All of us, gazing with unveiled face on the glory of the Lord, are being transformed into the same image from glory to glory, as from the Lord who is the Spirit. (2 Cor. 3:18)

I am the root and offspring of David, the bright morning star. (Rv. 22:16)

CHAPTER 8

THE RISEN CHRIST-CHRIST VICTORIOUS

Christianity exists as a religion, because of the Resurrection of Christ. The Resurrection is that important. The religious authorities and the Romans believed that an effective way to destroy a false prophet, religious movement or uprising, was to kill the prophet or the leader. It was usually that simple. But nothing about Jesus' life or mission was simple.

Though scholars disagree on whether the Sanhedrin, the supreme religious council, could sentence someone to death, it seems that before A.D. 200, they did have that authority. St. Stephen, who was a deacon in the early Church in Jerusalem, was stoned to death for blasphemy, after a trial by the Sanhedrin. (He is venerated as the first martyr in the Church.) According to the *Hebrew Scriptures*, a false messiah/prophet could be executed:

> *But if a prophet presumes to speak in my name an oracle that I have not commanded him to speak, or speaks in the name of other gods, he shall die (Deuteronomy 18:20).*

According to the gospel accounts, after Jesus was betrayed by Judas, he was arrested in the Garden of Gethsemane and brought before the Sanhedrin, for a first questioning. That meeting took place at night and was not a formal trial. The Sanhedrin was made up of the High Priest (who in that time period was appointed by the Romans), chief priests, elders and scribes. They tried to prove Jesus was a false prophet but failed to have the required agreement between two or three witnesses, which was necessary (see *Dt. 19:15*). The next morning, the interrogation continued. Again, Jesus was questioned by members of the Sanhedrin. Their jealousy and fear turned to anger when they began to question Jesus.

> *Again the High Priest asked him and said to him, 'Are you the Messiah, the Son of the Blessed One?' Jesus answered, 'I am; and you will see the Son of Man seated at the right hand of the Power and coming with the clouds of heaven' (Mk. 14:61-62).*

Jesus spoke of his coming glory. Much drama followed as Caiaphas, the High Priest *tore his garments* and cried: *'What further need have we of witnesses? You have heard the blasphemy. What do you think?'* *They all condemned him as deserving to die (Mark 14:61-64).* Blasphemy as related to Jesus' case, meant "claiming for oneself a dignity meant for God alone." (A fascinating fact about Caiaphas is that his tomb was found in 1990, during construction of a park in Jerusalem. Caiaphas is a rare name and scholars are convinced it is the tomb of the High Priest Caiaphas.)

The Sanhedrin agreed that Jesus was a false prophet as well as a false messiah/king. They clearly wanted Rome to conduct his public trial. As a false king, he would be a threat to Caesar and therefore be under the jurisdiction of Rome.

Jesus was mocked and then taken to Pontius Pilate, the Roman governor. Pilate was reluctant to get involved in religious disputes and sent Jesus to Herod Antipas, tetrarch of Galilee. Pilate believed Jesus was under his jurisdiction, as a Galilean. But Herod didn't want to get involved either and Jesus would not speak, so Herod further humiliated and mocked Jesus by placing an ornate robe on him and sent him back to Pilate.

At the governor's palace, Jesus was once more before Pilate. Frustrated by how the situation was unfolding, Pilate said to the Sanhedrin: *'Take him yourselves, and judge him according to your law' (John 18:31).* But when they refused, (they claimed not to have authority to execute Jesus), Pilate said to Jesus during the interrogation that followed, *'Are you the king of the Jews?'* Jesus replied, *'You say so.'* In St. John's gospel account, Jesus replies, *'My kingdom does not belong to this world...My kingdom is not here' (John 18:36).* Pilate responds, *'Then you are a king?'* Jesus says, *'You say I am a king, For this I was born and for this I came into the world to testify to the truth. Everyone who belongs to the truth listens to my voice.'* Pilate's answer is famous: *'What is truth?'* Jesus, it seems had unnerved Pilate and Pilate tells the Sanhedrin he finds no guilt in Jesus. Perhaps Pilate feared retribution from the gods, he didn't fully understand who he was dealing with. If Jesus was a false prophet, false god or a false messiah, he wasn't convinced any of those accusations warranted a horrific death.

> *Consequently, Pilate tried to release him but they cried, 'If you release him, you are not a friend of Caesar. Everyone who makes himself a king opposes Caesar' (John 19:12).*

The Sanhedrin were emphatic, they insisted Jesus was a threat to Caesar since he was making himself a king. Pilate then asked the crowd if he should release Jesus, as it was the custom to release one prisoner during religious feasts of importance. So Pilate said to the crowd: *'Do you want me to release to you the king of the Jews?' (John 18:39).*

But the crowd was incited to ask for Barabbas' release instead. So Pilate said: '*Then what do you want me to do with the man you call the king of the Jews?*' *They shouted,* '*Crucify him!*' But Pilate resisted, asking the crowd, '*What evil has he done?*' The crowd could not be placated. Evil intentions, the distortion of evil rage and sinfulness had taken over the crowd. They shouted, '*Crucify him!*'

The charges against Jesus were serious and the religious authorities were firm in their accusations against Jesus and in the end, they couldn't be ignored. The false accusations were upheld. Jesus, according to the Sanhedrin, had subverted the nation by stirring up trouble, he opposed paying taxes to Caesar, he claimed to forgive sins (which only God could do), and claimed he was divine –*The Father and I are one......The Father is in me and I am in the Father (John 10:30, 38).* As a "messiah/king" Jesus was supposedly a threat to Caesar.

As recorded only in *The Gospel of Matthew*, Pilate washed his hands, a symbolic action, to show he did not want to be held responsible for Jesus' death. As he washed his hands, he said to the crowd, '*I am innocent of this man's blood; see to it yourselves*' *(Mt. 27:24).* (Though Pilate would wash his hands, Christians would never forget his role in condemning Jesus to death and crucifying him. In two ancient Trinitarian creeds of the Church, the Nicene Creed and the Apostles' Creed, Pilate's involvement in Jesus' death is stated. In the Nicene Creed which is recited during the Mass by the entire congregation, Catholics proclaim in unison: *And in Jesus Christ, his only Son our Lord.....suffered under Pontius Pilate, was crucified, died and was buried.* Also in the Apostles' Creed, which is used for catechetical purposes and also recited as part of the recitation of the Rosary, Pilate's name is mentioned in connection with Jesus' death: *.....born of the Virgin Mary, suffered under Pontius Pilate, was crucified, died and was buried.....* Pilate washed his hands but his infamous involvement in Jesus' death lives on in creeds that are recited to this day, everyday, throughout the world.)

Jesus was sentenced to death. He would suffer a humiliating and painful death on a Cross, the Romans would execute him in a barbaric way. He would be crucified alongside criminals. One of them would ask him: *'Jesus remember me when you come into your kingdom.'* Jesus responded: *'Today you will be with me in Paradise' (Luke 23:42-43).*

He would be treated with scorn and contempt and many of the prophecies of Isaiah about the "Suffering Servant" would be fulfilled:

> *I gave my back to those who beat me, my cheeks to those who plucked my beard; my face I did not shield from buffets and spitting (Is. 50:6).*

In John's gospel, it is written: *When the soldiers had crucified Jesus, they took his clothes and divided them into four shares, a share for each soldier. They also took his tunic, but the tunic was seamless, woven in one piece from the top down.* So they said:

'*let's not tear it but cast lots for it to see whose it will be*' (*John 19:23-24*). Scholars have noted that John mentioned the seamless tunic for a specific reason. A seamless robe or tunic, according to the ancient Israelite tradition, was worn by Adam, Moses and High Priests. It was forbidden to tear a High Priest's tunic (see *Leviticus 21:10*). St. John wants the early Christians to recognize Jesus as the Great High Priest, who wore a seamless tunic.

Death could not hold Jesus. The tomb could not hold him. Jesus was not a subversive criminal or a false messiah, he was innocent of all the charges brought against him. He was who He said He was. His kingdom was not of this world. He was truly the Savior of the world and the long-awaited Messiah who the Hebrew prophets had spoken of, in the years and centuries before his birth. His Resurrection would usher in the Messianic Age and a new everlasting covenant.

> *Now in Christ Jesus you who once were far off have become near by the blood of Christ (Eph. 2:13)....... So then you are no longer strangers and sojourners, but you are fellow citizens with the holy ones and members of the household of God, built upon the foundation of the apostles and prophets, with Christ Jesus himself as the capstone. (Eph. 2:19-20).*

(It is important to note here a fact that is sometimes overlooked or understated. Jesus was Jewish as well as his mother Mary and foster-father Joseph, Elizabeth and Zechariah, (John the Baptist's parents) and of course John the Baptist and his other relatives as well. The apostles and many of his closest followers were also Jewish. The religious authorities in power, most especially the Sanhedrin, who were blinded to who Jesus was and feared him, were responsible for "handing Jesus over" to the Romans. It is important to note that distinction. The ancient Romans were ultimately those in power, who were responsible for the execution of Jesus.)

The *Hebrew Scriptures* filled with the prophecies of the ancient Hebrew prophets concerning the coming Messiah's birth, teachings, suffering and death would be fulfilled in Christ, according to Christian belief and teachings. This powerful prophecy would be fulfilled in Christ:

> *For a child is born to us; a son is given to us; upon his shoulders dominion rests. They name him Wonder-Counselor, God-Hero, Father-Forever, Prince of Peace. His dominion is vast and forever peaceful, from David's throne and over his kingdom, which he confirms and sustains by judgment and justice, both now and forever (Isaiah 9:5-6).*

Christians believe that when Mary, the mother of Jesus was told by the archangel Gabriel that she had *found favor with God and she should not be afraid,* Isaiah's prophecy would be fulfilled, in the coming supernatural events. At the Annunciation (announcement), Gabriel declared to Mary:

> *You shall conceive and bear a son and give him the name Jesus. Great will be his dignity and he will be called the Son of the Most High. The Lord God will give him the throne of David his father. He will rule over the House of Jacob forever and his reign will be without end (Luke: 31-33).*

Though Mary was puzzled, the angel told her: *Nothing is impossible with God.* An empowering statement that should give all of us hope and courage, in uncertain situations. Mary humbly accepted her role in salvation history with her famous reply: *I am the servant of the Lord. Let it be done to me as you say.* And so God's plan unfolded with Mary's fiat, her "yes" to God's plan. She was a young, holy, receptive woman of deep prayer, specially chosen by God to be the vessel, which would bring the Davidic-Messiah into the world, thus fulfilling Isaiah's prophecies and other prophecies as well. We too are called to be holy vessels to help bring forth the Reign of God and do our part in salvation history.

Many of Isaiah's prophecies, would be the fulfilled in Jesus, as well as this one:

> *I, the Lord, have called you for the victory of justice, I have grasped you by the hand; I formed you and set*

you as a covenant of the people, a light for the nations. To open the eyes of the blind, to bring out prisoners from confinement, and from the dungeon those who live in darkness.... (Isaiah 42:6-7)

Jesus said: I am the light of the world. Whoever follows me will not walk in darkness, but will have the light of life (John 8:12).

Jesus of Nazareth was God Incarnate and the religious leaders and the Roman authorities were not prepared for what happened after the crucifixion. For the Romans, all their expertise in matters of conquering, occupying, quelling rebellions or defiant acts against the Empire or remaining in control of situations, were no match for God's plan, for the Resurrection of Christ. As Pope Benedict XVI wrote in his book, "Jesus of Nazareth-Holy Week: From the Entrance into Jerusalem to the Resurrection," *The Christian faith stands or falls with the truth of the testimony that Christ is risen from the dead.....Only if Jesus is risen has anything really new occurred that changes the world and the situation of mankind. Then he becomes the criterion on which we can rely. For then God has truly revealed himself (pp.241-242).* That is so true. We can rely on the Resurrection and the witness accounts of the apostles and disciples of Christ. God revealed the mystery of Christ, in all its fullness and depth to the early apostles, disciples and followers of Jesus. God revealed through the Resurrection how

He can turn despair, suffering and loss- what seemed like the utter powerlessness of Jesus at the Crucifixion into glory, new life and the miracle of the Resurrection. In the early Church, belief in the Resurrection was central to being a follower of Christ, a disciple of "the Way." All four gospels have accounts of the Resurrection, though they differ in some ways, they all express a deep belief in the Resurrection. They all begin by mentioning an empty tomb. It is mentioned in the teachings and *Letters of St. Paul* and it is contained in *The Acts of the Apostles.*

God raised this Jesus; of this we are all witnesses, exalted at the right hand of God, he received the promise of the Holy Spirit from the Father and poured it forth, as you both see and hear (Acts 2:32-33).

The early Church gave Jesus the title, "Kyrios" (Lord) to stress that He was equal to God. The early Christians professed with certainty and confidence, that Jesus was Lord.

For if you confess with your mouth that Jesus is Lord and believe in your heart that God raised him from the dead, you will be saved (Romans 10:9).

The Resurrection was a pivotal event in the history of humankind. It was an historic event. Jesus' Resurrection changed the course of human history, it was that important. It remains so over two thousand years later, for over two billion Christians throughout the world.

The first Easter morning began with an empty tomb, according to eyewitnesses.

> *On the first day of the week, at dawn, the women came to the tomb bringing the spices they had prepared. They found the stone rolled back from the tomb; but when they entered the tomb, they did not find the body of the Lord Jesus. While they were still at a loss over what to think of this, two men in dazzling garments stood beside them. Terrified, the women bowed to the ground. The men said to them: ' Why do you search for the Living One among the dead? He is not here; he has been raised up. Remember what he said to you while you were in Galilee-that the Son of Man must be delivered into the hands of sinful men and be crucified and on the third day rise again.' With this reminder, his words came back to them' (Luke 24:1-8).*

From St. Matthew's gospel we have this account:

> *After the Sabbath, as the first day of the week was dawning, Mary Magdalene and the other Mary came to see the tomb. And behold, there was a great earthquake, for an angel of the Lord descended from Heaven, approached and rolled back the stone and sat upon it. His appearance was like lightning and his clothing was white as snow....*

Then the angel said to the women, 'Do not be afraid! I know you are seeking Jesus the crucified. He is not here, for he has been raised just as he said. Come and see the place where he lay.' Then go quickly and tell his disciples, 'He has been raised from the dead and he is going before you to Galilee, there you will see him' (see Mt. 28:1-7).

In Matthew's account what follows is unique to his gospel account. Jesus appears to the women, as they are traveling and they were given a special grace to recognize him, in this post-resurrection account. They embrace his feet and begin to praise him. Jesus tells them: *'Do not be afraid. Go tell my brothers to go to Galilee and there they will see me' (Matt. 28:9-10).* Jesus had a body that they could embrace, he was not a ghostly figure. Their imagination was not playing tricks on them. Though the experience must have had a dream-like quality, the extraordinary events happened as the women proclaimed, and the realization of a Risen Christ, a supernatural occurrence, would begin to take hold among Jesus' followers and give them hope and courage.

Jesus rose from the dead, as he predicted he would. He would appear, after his Resurrection, to his apostles and disciples, who didn't always recognize him immediately. In many accounts, after He rose, He would not be recognized at first, so it is assumed His appearance was transformed. His appearance must have been slightly different after He rose from the dead. His glorified body perhaps showed his divinity to a greater degree, (though he remained fully human and fully divine).

According to St. John's gospel account, Mary Magdalene who stood outside the tomb weeping only recognized Jesus, when he called her name. A transformation had taken place but it's not exactly clear what that change was. (See *John 20:11-16*).

In Luke's gospel story about Jesus appearing after his Resurrection in his glorified state, Luke tells of two disciples walking on the road to Emmaus, sad and disillusioned. They are returning home to their village of Emmaus, after witnessing the puzzling events that happened in Jerusalem. They have heard rumors of an empty tomb and a vision of angels saying Jesus was alive but they are still confused about the events of the previous days. Jesus appears suddenly and joins them but they don't recognize him, at first. They converse with him and find it hard to believe that the stranger who has joined them hasn't heard the news about Jesus' death. Jesus said to them:

> *Oh, how foolish you are and how slow of heart to believe all that the prophets have declared. Was it not necessary that the Messiah should suffer these things and then enter into his glory? Then beginning with Moses and all the prophets, he interpreted to them the things about himself in all the Scriptures (Luke 24:25-27).*

Yet, it was only after Jesus, began the ritual, that they realized who He was.

> *He took bread, pronounced the blessing, broke the bread and began to distribute it to them, that their eyes were fully opened and they realized it was Jesus. Jesus vanished but they said to each other, 'Were not our hearts burning inside us as he talked to us on the road and explained the Scriptures to us?' (Luke 24:30-32).*

The two disciples quickly returned to Jerusalem to tell the others what they had experienced. They could not contain their excitement or joy, for the Lord had appeared to them in the "breaking of the bread."

Jesus also appeared suddenly, in a room where the doors were locked, he came into their midst and said to them: *'Peace be with you.' When he had said this, he showed them his hands and his side. The disciples rejoiced when they saw the Lord (John 20:19-22).* Once again, he said, *'Peace be with you.'* He added an important component. He was going to send them out to do God's work in the world, but he empowered them, for the task.

> *'As the Father has sent me, so I send you.' And then he breathed on them and invoked the Holy Spirit and asked them to be receptive to receiving the power of God, Jesus proclaimed, 'Receive the Holy Spirit!'*

Another extraordinary post-Resurrection appearance happened on the Sea of Tiberias. Peter, along with some of the apostles went fishing, but caught nothing. When it was dawn, Jesus was standing on the shore, but again he was not recognized. He called to them and asked if they had anything to eat. When they replied "no" he told them to cast the net over the right side of the boat. It was then that they caught a great number of fish. Their eyes were "opened" and the Beloved Disciple said to Peter: *'It is the Lord' (John 21:7)*. Peter was overwhelmed with emotion and impulsively jumped into the sea. Remarkably, Jesus ate breakfast with them.

According to Scripture, Jesus appeared to the disciples for forty days. He told the disciples that they would be his *witnesses in Jerusalem, in all Judea and Samaria, and to the ends of the earth (Acts 1:8)*. He told them to wait in Jerusalem. *'Remain in the city until you are clothed with power from on high' (Luke 24:49)*. Then according to St. Luke: *As they were looking on, he was lifted up and a cloud took him from their sight (Acts 1:9)*. Jesus ascended into Heaven before their eyes. The Ascension is also mentioned in 1Peter 3:22, ….*through the Resurrection of Jesus Christ, who has gone into Heaven and is at the right hand of God, with angels, authorities, and powers subject to him.*

The Feast of Harvest or Feast of Weeks was a Jewish harvest festival. Israelites would travel to Jerusalem for the feast to bring the first fruits of the harvest as an offering to God. Jerusalem would be very crowded with pilgrims and there would be a celebratory mood in the holy city. There were special offerings and sacrifices especially for that day. The High Priest would make a special offering to God of two loaves of baked wheat bread. Jesus' apostles and disciples were also in Jerusalem, but they were there waiting for the outpouring of the "holy power" that Jesus promised to send to them, after he ascended. According to *The Acts of the Apostles*, as they all prayed together in the Upper Room,

> *Suddenly there came from the sky a noise like a strong driving wind and it filled the entire house... then there appeared to them tongues of fire, which parted and came to rest on each one of them. They were filled with the Holy Spirit and began to speak in different tongues as the Spirit enabled them to proclaim (Acts 2:1-4).*

The disciples were then filled with courage, determination and confidence. They were emboldened and empowered by the Holy Spirit. They were unstoppable! Peter boldly spoke to a large crowd about Jesus and finished by stating:

> *'Therefore let the whole house of Israel know for certain that God has made him both Lord and Messiah, this Jesus whom you crucified' (Acts 2:36).*

The Feast of Pentecost for Christians began that day, during the Jewish Feast of Harvest, with the powerful and visible outpouring of the Holy Spirit in the holy city, Jerusalem. It is often referred to as, "the birthday of the church." The ancient church, the community of believers began that holy day. As a biblical scholar once told me, "The early Christians were so filled with joy and the Spirit, they were dancing in the streets."

In writing to the people of Corinth, a Christian community that St. Paul had established about the year A.D. 51, he would stress in his letter that after Jesus rose from the dead, he appeared not only to Peter and the Twelve, but he *appeared to more than five hundred brothers, at once, most of whom are still living... (1 Cor. 15:5)*. St. Paul, as a great preacher and evangelizer, was firm in his belief, that the early Christian communities must have deep faith and belief in the Resurrection of Christ. He also makes clear to the Corinthians: *If Christ has not been raised, your faith is in vain (1 Cor. 15:17)*.

St. Paul would suffer much for his belief in Jesus and the Resurrection.

They stoned Paul and dragged him out of the city, supposing that he was dead. (Acts 14:19b). Much to their surprise he was not dead. Paul would have many harrowing experiences and suffer much for his belief in the Resurrection. According to ancient sources and tradition, Paul was beheaded by the Romans in about the year A.D. 65.

(It is interesting to note that historians who study that time period in history say that there is no logical reason why Christianity spread as quickly as it did throughout the Roman Empire and the world. It is true that the Emperor Constantine legalized Christianity in the Roman Empire about the year A.D. 313, (after he had a religious experience and won a battle that he attributed to God's intercession) and the persecution of Christians stopped. They were then allowed to freely worship and assemble and the building of churches began. Of course, that helped Christianity to flourish, but from a religious viewpoint, a more important reason is because of the coming of the Holy Spirit at Pentecost, which empowered the apostles and disciples of Christ to go out fearlessly and preach the good news. Christians believe that to be true. It is also important to note that Jesus was a compelling figure, who inspired people and gave them hope and purpose. His words and teachings had a power of their own.)

What can all this possibly have to do with me? As I've mentioned before, I am a baptized Catholic Christian, living in the modern world, in seemingly ordinary circumstances. I do take my faith very seriously. I'm a person of prayer. I love God. I'm on a spiritual journey. I continue to study, take courses, go on retreats and even give lectures and retreats on the Christian faith, but that is not anything unusual. Many other people, religious and laypeople do that. But what is unusual is that I am writing in this book that I saw, one evening, many years ago, a vision of the Risen Christ in a Catholic Church in Brooklyn. Just like that as I've written before, he appeared suddenly. Dressed in a fine vestment and a miter-like head covering, he was present suddenly, quietly, without fanfare or ceremony. Just like that. It's hard to believe, I know it is, but that is my reality, that is what happened to me. You can believe it or dismiss it, as you like. But I can't. It changed my life, it changed my worldview, I could never be the same. Strangely and mysteriously, during those surreal, extraordinary moments, I was given proof of the existence of God, the existence of another dimension, the divinity of Christ, the Resurrection and proof of what the disciples and apostles said about Jesus' post-Resurrection appearances. As the apostles and disciples reported, spoke and wrote about, He can appear out of nowhere, He can come through walls or locked doors. He can appear suddenly and then vanish quickly. Without fanfare or angels or saints surrounding him, he can just appear, alone and fully in control. I hope I have in the past chapters of this book, explained why I think it was an authentic religious experience. It's up to you to decide what you think about it. Either way, I hope you've learned something from my observations and/or my research. I wish to convey: God is real, Jesus is the Messiah, he did resurrect from the dead, He is who He said He was, He gives new life and freedom to anyone who calls upon His Holy Name. He is the "Great Forgiver," the "Merciful One" and the "Divine Physician." He is full of humility, mercy and love. He is: *the Way, the Truth and the Life.* If you haven't yet discovered the depth of meaning, purpose and fulfillment that being in relationship with Christ brings, I assure you, He is waiting for you, to approach Him and pray to Him. *Behind and before you encircle me and rest your hand upon me (Psalm 139:5).*

Christ is patient, He waits with love to "to quench your thirst" and make you whole. *All of you who are thirsty, come to the water! (Is. 55:1)* As Christ fulfilled: *Let anyone who thirsts come to me and drink (John 7:37).* In the *Hebrew Scriptures,* from *The Book of Ezekiel,* the image of water *flowing out from beneath the threshold of the Temple toward the east (Ez. 47:1),* that turns into a river, provides an abundance of trees and fruit. *Along both banks of the river, fruit trees of every kind shall grow; their leaves shall not fade nor their fruit fail (Ez. 47:12).* Jesus who ushered in the Messianic Age, became the new Temple, the source of life-giving water. The "water" that flows from Jesus provides an abundance of life, goodness and refreshment. The connection between Jesus and life-giving water is once again reinforced in the following passages from *The Book of Revelation:*

> *Then the angel showed me the river of life-giving water, sparkling like crystal, flowing from the throne of God and of the Lamb.... (Book of Revelation 21:1).*

The Spirit and the bride say, 'Come.' Let the hearer say, 'Come.' Let the one who thirsts come forward, and the one who wants it, receive the gift of life-giving water (Rv. 22:17).

Our response should be joyful. Showing joy, being hopeful and giving praise to God because Jesus is truly the Savior of the world and the Christ. Though we don't know all the answers, and there are great mysteries woven into the Christian faith, Jesus' teachings and promises are true. In the end, as Julian of Norwich, (the English anchorite and mystic), proclaimed: "All will be well and all shall be well and all manner of thing will be well." Christians are to be people of hope, even in the midst of uncertainty, confusion and despair. The Resurrection and the outpouring of the Spirit- the fulfillment of the promises of Christ, are reasons enough to always remain in hope and expectation of the coming Reign of God.

After Jesus ascended and the apostles and disciples were empowered by the Holy Spirit, they remembered Jesus' teachings and commands and they began to act upon them. They had no fear, only confidence that they had been chosen by God, to do their part in God's plan and fulfill their role in salvation history. Before ascending, Christ challenged his apostles and followers to act on his words, to be holy, to help the poor and marginalized, to give of themselves in acts of mercy and charity.

They were to remain humble, be courageous and give freely. Most importantly, they were to devote themselves to the "communal life" and the "breaking of bread and prayers." And that is what they did.

Every day they devoted themselves to meeting together in the temple area and to breaking bread in their homes. They ate their meals with exultation and sincerity of heart, praising God and enjoying favor with all the people. And everyday the Lord added to their number those who were being saved (Acts 2:46-47). (Breaking of bread is what the early Christians called Eucharist or Holy Communion and they were following Jesus' command to, "Do this in memory of me.")

St. Paul, on his missionary journeys kept instructing and encouraging the early Christian communities through visits and letters. He exhorted the converts to be true to the calling they had received. He would write to the Galatians these powerful words, which he had internalized: *'I have been crucified with Christ; yet I live, no longer I, but Christ lives in me'…. (Gal. 2:19b-20a).* He believed he should be considered an apostle because he had seen a vision of the risen Christ. He began his letter to the Galatians stressing the point:

> *Paul an apostle, not from human beings nor through a human being but through Jesus Christ and God the Father, who raised him from the dead (Gal. 1:1).*

The letter he wrote to the Romans is considered a masterpiece. It is Paul's longest letter. Writing from Greece, Paul addressed the Christian community in Rome, with words that show how he had attained a deep understanding of Christ's message and how it "took hold of him." These are the words St. Paul wrote:

Let love be sincere, hate what is evil, hold onto what is good. Love one another with mutual affection; anticipate one another in showing honor. Do not grow slack in zeal, be fervent in spirit, serve the Lord. Rejoice in hope, endure in affliction, persevere in prayer. Contribute to the needs of the holy ones, exercise hospitality. Bless those who persecute you, bless and do not curse them. Rejoice with those who rejoice, weep with those who weep. Have the same regard for one another, do not be haughty but associate with the lowly; do not be wise in your own estimation.....Do not be conquered by evil but conquer evil with good (Romans 12:9-16,21).

These words are still relevant today and can enrich all of our lives and help us to be better human beings. Paul's words are powerful and moving. They had the power to transform and convert the readers and listeners, which is why Paul was such an effective evangelizer.

In writing to the Colossians, in Asia Minor, which was east of Ephesus, (modern day Turkey), Paul exhorted the early Christians to be Christ-like in their attitudes and to be true to the values Jesus taught. He begged them to live knowing they had the power of the Holy Spirit, and to turn away from anything that was not from God. Paul was writing from prison. His words challenge us, even today, to live according to higher truths:

> *Put on then, as God's chosen ones, holy and beloved, heartfelt compassion, kindness, humility, gentleness, and patience, bearing with one another and forgiving one another, if one has a grievance against another; as the Lord has forgiven you, so must you also do. And over all these put on love, that is, the bond of perfection (Colossians 3:12-14).*

St. Paul, in his letters stressed the importance of love. Jesus' teachings on love had captured his religious imagination and changed his life and so he never tired of reminding his readers of its importance.

> *Love is patient, love is kind. It is not jealous, love is not pompous, it is not inflated, it is not rude, it does not seek its own interests, it is not quick-tempered, it does not brood over injury. It does not rejoice over wrongdoing but rejoices with the truth. It bears all*

things, believes all things, hopes all things, endures all things (1 Cor. 13:4-7).

Love is the essence of the *New Testament* and the foundation of Jesus' teachings. God's essence is love. As St. John wrote: *God is love.* According to St. Paul, *...love is the fulfillment of the law (Rom. 13:10).*

In St. Matthew's gospel, Jesus tells his disciples that they are to love their enemies and pray for those who persecute them. It is a radical teaching, then and now and not easy to follow. But that is what is required to be "perfect." Jesus' command: *Be perfect just as your heavenly Father is perfect (Mt. 5:48),* is only found in St. Matthew's gospel. That is the ideal, that is what Christians try to strive for, to be truly good, whole, and as "perfect" as possible in this earthly life. It is something which can take a lifetime to achieve. One step at a time, one day at a time, examining our conscience at the end of each day, staying on track, being faithful to spiritual disciplines and taking advantage of all the Church offers to bring us closer to God. Through Christian meditation, prayer, the sacraments and reflection on Scripture, we can grow nearer to God and come to know God's will for us.

> *Do not conform yourself to this age but be transformed by the renewal of your mind, that you may discern what is the will of God, what is good and pleasing and perfect (Romans 12:2).*

We will gain much if we are receptive and open to the power and guidance of the Holy Spirit. We are called to trust in God and the abundance of God's grace and mercy and keep our eyes fixed on Jesus, at all times and in all situations. Our gaze should always be towards Christ.

Prayer is a great gift and a blessing. We cannot do it alone, there is too much uncertainty in the modern world. Prayer helps us keep our priorities straight and focused on what's really important in life. Prayer also helps us to depend on God and open ourselves to God's mercy, grace and favor. *Blessed are they who put their trust in God (Ps. 2:12b).*

Just as Jesus prayed at important times during his life, we too, must realize that prayer helps, heals and makes a difference, in our relationship with God and others. Through his teachings, Jesus taught his disciples to be persistent in prayer and never give up. It is important to pray for those we love, through intercessory prayer, which can be very powerful.

It is good to pray for the marginalized, the poor and for world peace. And to pray, as the saints' did, to know the will of God. The simplest and yet most powerful prayer is: "Come, Holy Spirit! Veni, Sanctus Spiritus!" Say it often and open yourself to the transforming power of God.

...He breathed on them and said to them, 'Receive the Holy Spirit!' (John 20:220)

Also, in times of trouble, doubt, despair, uncertainty and trial the simple yet highly effective words from St. Faustina's revelations, "Jesus, I trust in you," will be a source of comfort, stability and power. Over and over again, "Jesus, I trust in you!"

Jesus commanded and commissioned his apostles and disciples, with these words, (they are for us today as well),

> *Go therefore and make disciples of all nations, baptizing them in the name of the Father and of the Son and of the Holy Spirit, teaching them to observe all that I have commanded you. And behold, I am with you always, until the end of the age (Matthew 28:19-20).*

And never forget: *You are a chosen race, a royal priesthood, a holy nation, a people of his own, so that you may announce the praises of him who called you out of darkness into his wonderful light (1 Peter 2:9).*

You are a new creation in Christ. *So whoever is in Christ is a new creation: the old things have passed away; behold, new things have come (2 Cor. 5:17).*

> *I have loved you, says the Lord (Malachi 1:2).*

Amen! So Be It!

ABOUT THE AUTHOR

N. J. Azzaro, MS, lives on Long Island, New York, but has taught both preschool and high school religion in Brooklyn as well as serving as a director of religious education in a Brooklyn parish. She earned a master's degree from Fordham University's School of Religion and Religious Education. She is actively involved in her local civic association and is a current member and former vice President and president of the "Friends of the Seminary," a volunteer-based group for the Seminary of the Immaculate Conception in Huntington, Long Island. She continues to serve her parish as a prayer leader for the children's liturgy program. She also spends time serving as a retreat leader and lecturer. This is her first book. You can follow her blog at brooklyn-born-believer.blogspot.com.

51510762R00110

Made in the USA
Middletown, DE
11 November 2017